Hero or Coward

PRESSURES FACING THE SOLDIER IN BATTLE

Elmar Dinter

FRANK CASS

First Published 1985 in Great Britain by
FRANK CASS AND COMPANY LIMITED
Gainsborough House, 11 Gainsborough Road,
London, E11 1RS, England

and in the United States of America by
FRANK CASS AND COMPANY LIMITED
c/o Biblio Distribution Centre
81 Adams Drive, P.O. Box 327, Totowa, N.J. 07511

Copyright © 1985 Elmar Dinter

British Library Cataloguing in Publication Data

Dinter, Elmar
  Hero or coward.
  1. War—Psychological aspects
  I. Title   II. Held oder Feigling. *English*
  355'.02'019   U22.3

  ISBN 0-7146-3230-9

Typeset by Williams Graphics, Abergele, North Wales.
Printed in Great Britain by
A. Wheaton & Co. Ltd., Exeter

Contents

1   Introduction   1

2   Setting The Scene   6

3   Stress   13

4   Pressures on the Individual   16

5   Injury and Death   22

6   Stamina and Exhaustion   27

7   Firepower   34

8   Experiences of Military Units   40

9   Experiences of Commanders   52

10   Summary of Pressures   60

11   Psychiatric Casualties   63

12   Summary of Antidotes   71

13   Effects on the Commander   80

14   Consequences for Personnel Selection, Organization, Equipment, Training, Education, Leadership and Tactics   87

15   Future Prospects   112

16   Open Questions   125

17   Conclusion   129

Selected Bibliography   133

Appendix A   Introduction to the Historical Examples   137

Appendix B   The Battle for Calais   140

Appendix C   The Battle for Stalingrad   153

Appendix D   The Battle for Monte Cassino   173

Acknowledgements

I received a great deal of help in the preparation of this book and I should like to mention especially:

The Staff College, Camberley, which under the command of Major General D.B. Alexander-Sinclair and his deputy Brigadier J.B. Bettridge constantly provided me with fresh inspiration.

Its Librarian, Mike Sims who helped me considerably with the translation and editing of the English version.

His predecessor Ken White who with his staff helped me to obtain source material.

My wife Ulrike, and Tricia Hughes who prepared the German and English manuscripts respectively.

Enid Martin and Sheena Lill of the Staff College Work Production Centre, who prepared the illustrations.

The Directing Staff and students of the Staff College who assisted me with their helpful discussions.

And, last but not least, my sons Christian and Tim who suffered with equanimity the fact that their father, for many months, spent his spare time reading and writing and not with them.

I am indebted to them all and it is to them that this book is dedicated.

Elmar Dinter

CHAPTER ONE

Introduction

For every soldier without battle experience, the question of how he would react to the physical and psychological pressures of war is both fascinating and frightening. The thoughts and emotions which this question evokes are similar to those of mountain climbers on a rock face, or of ocean sailors who have got themselves involved in an adventure which, in spite of the excitement, has dangerous aspects.

Even though the average soldier will not seek battles, and even if war, with its terrors for combatants and non-combatants alike, can hardly be described as an adventure, the individual in the fighting is faced with the same challenge as men engaged in an adventure: that of proving himself. He may well ask: 'Will I emerge from the battle as a hero or as a coward?'

Even when talking to soldiers with battle experience it becomes evident that they too ask themselves the same question over and over again. Although they are aware that their successful performance can be counted as a positive experience, they are aware too that they must always prove themselves anew and that every battle will involve new terrors.

Even for those who have never served in the armed forces and do not intend to do so, this question is both fascinating and disturbing, because the answer to it aims very quickly at the deep conscious and unconscious 'inner self', past the somewhat shallow terms of 'hero' and 'coward'. In this investigation of the inner self, one almost feels like a potholer, who would love to know where the labyrinth of passages and caves will lead him and what it contains, but knows that each step takes him ever further from the apparent safety of the surface.

The answer to the question is not only intriguing and exciting for the individual, but is the decisive criterion for the selection of personnel, the organization, equipment, training, education, leadership and tactics of armed forces.

If, for example, the dominating role of the small group is demonstrated, the organization must take it into account. If noise is an above average pressure, this could be allowed for in the development of weapons and equipment. If lack of understanding in certain fields results in additional nervous strain, the subjects studied and the time allocated for training should be altered. If formal discipline provides definite moral support in battle, it should be part of a soldier's training; and if the pressures the leader faces are different from those of his men, this will affect personnel selection. This should suffice as an indication – the subject is dealt with at length later in the book.

Because of the importance of this topic to the military leader, this book is directed at him rather than at the scientist, and discussions of a technical nature such as the distinction between fear and anxieties are avoided as far as possible.

There will be many answers to our question. Nothing is gained by listing them all; this would only highlight conflicting requirements some of which could not be realized. Some would be contradictory. Others might be too expensive or run counter to the ethics of society.

Therefore, it is essential that the different pressures and their consequences should not only be enumerated, but should be compared, weighed and placed in an order of priority. This is the main aim of this study.

Let us consider, for example, possible consequences for the organization of the armed forces. If group cohesion proves to be important, this might require the setting up and maintenance of stable groups. However, there are also justifiable demands for movement of personnel, and this becomes particularly important in battle. It is equally vital for leaders, who can broaden their experience only in this way. Movement also makes it possible for ambitious soldiers to get promotion, and it ensures adequate replacements. It may also assist in the admission of women in order to achieve equality. All these points of view must be taken into account. Mere listing would be of little value. Only comparative assessment will get us any further.

Thus it is not merely a case of investigating what weighs on the soldier in time of war; what matters is to find out the decisive pressures and then to set out the conclusions in some order.

Finally, it is helpful to disclose to the soldiers themselves the answers to this question. With a full knowledge of what they can expect in war, soldiers without battle experience are in a better position to control their own reactions. By taking appropriate measures, commanders are able to reduce the effects of the pressures. Here, too, knowledge is helpful. It prepares the individual and the group for battle conditions. The terrors are depressing enough. Almost everyone will try to avoid them, but if this is not possible, they are more bearable this way.

Many attempts have been made to answer this important question, especially in the field which the West German Armed Forces call 'Innere Führung' (civic education and leadership). Their value cannot be denied, but most of them concentrate on the ethical aspects. They examine the importance of political education and law and order, deal with democratic and totalitarian systems, assess aggression and defence preparedness, or advise on the soldiers' welfare. But no one attempts to explain in a comprehensive and unbiased way why some people are brave and others cowardly. Nor, of course, can anyone draw any conclusions regarding armed forces. The answer to our question may also revive the important discussion about 'Innere Führung'.

Anyone who attempts an answer will have to revise many of the cherished opinions with which he has surrounded himself like a protective screen. He will also encounter limits. The 'cave' will disclose 'side-passages' which we cannot penetrate at present.

He will also be exposed to extremes of feeling, because on the one hand he will be affected by the experiences described by combatants, and on the other hand he must assess the events dispassionately and from a distance – apparently heartlessly.

This is a burden which can only be borne with good will.

As has already been indicated, the literature provides quite a number of answers. Fiction, whether imaginative or based on experience, has a penchant for this subject, because the possibilities for dramatic treatment and embellishment of a warlike situation can hardly be improved upon, and it is possible to wallow in sentiment. At the same time statements made in some of these works should not be dismissed. Many of them provide clearer, less ambiguous and above all more penetrating answers than many academic works are able to do. Their disadvantage lies in the fact that they are not written with the aim of answering our question comprehensively and factually. They illuminate only selected aspects and these are then highlighted with reference to a specific situation. So the appropriate novel is of quite some importance to us, but it should not be taken as a ground for generalization.

Scientific literature on this subject is not particularly extensive in Germany. Some of these works, such as Freud's *Zeitgemässes über Krieg und Tod* or Marshall's *Men against Fire* and some of the more popular works by Biglar (*Der einsame Soldat*) or by Schneider (*Das Buch vom Soldaten*) have lost none of the force of their arguments over the years.

In the English language, on the other hand, there is a surprising number of books and articles dealing with the pressures experienced by soldiers in battle. The Americans in particular provide extensive material, part of which moulders, little used, in archives and libraries. They are veritable mines of information. *The American Soldier* with about 2,500 pages is a good example. Unfortunately these books too only give partial answers.

This is because, as in fiction, attention is often concentrated on a few aspects. This may be because it is intended to emphasize a single essential idea. Moreover it is only too obvious in some works that, in spite of the appearance of scholarship, the writer has not found it possible to eliminate the influence of his own cultural background.

In addition, there are several new scientific discoveries on stress which have not yet been taken into account in such books. Nevertheless, scientific literature on this subject provides a solid basis for any further investigation. For this book too, it provided an essential indication of where research should start.

Further insights were gained by interviewing certain selected combatants who, because of their education, should have been in a position to provide a well-reasoned assessment. But even the statements by soldiers who had taken part in battle over a long period of time, and who therefore had considerable personal experience, provided no satisfactory solution. We know how difficult it is to remain objective, particularly when one's own anxieties are involved. It was also noticeable that even the experience provided by 'old soldiers' was only one piece in a jigsaw puzzle, because of the many variations which every battle offers.

It was this realization that finally gave this book its shape. On the one hand it demanded intensive historical study. On the other, a comprehensive assessment of the scientific literature – unfortunately a very painstaking and time-consuming procedure, but the only means of establishing the correctness and completeness of its conclusions and of weighing one against another to obtain an accurate picture.

The author would not expect every reader to take a similar tortuous path, but for those wishing to do so, selected quotations are included in the appendices and are referred to throughout the text in order to illustrate the various arguments.

In the first part of the book the experiences of the combatants are summarized and analysed, mainly from a psychological point of view, making use of the available scientific literature. Only then is it possible to investigate what can be done in detail in order to counter the pressures of battle, and we can then ask ourselves to what special influences a leader is subjected. Here, therefore, an attempt is made to provide an answer to our central question – why one soldier emerges from battle as a hero and the other as a coward. In the last part of the book, possibly the most important one, conclusions are drawn with regard to personnel selection, organization, equipment, training, education and leadership, right down to small-scale tactics.

It was not always possible to give a definitive answer to all the questions. Nevertheless an attempt has been made in all the important areas to provide at least an indication of trends, whilst pointing out all the doubts and contradictions.

The references to the literature have been selective, with a view to encouraging meaningful reading. In some areas it was difficult to find easily accessible published material. In such cases the permission of the persons concerned was obtained to use their findings as confirmation of the author's observations. A reference to the actual documents was not possible.

Finally, an attempt is made to describe a possible future war scenario, and it becomes evident that in some areas even an indication of trends is impossible because of the absence of documentation and research. These are the areas in which further investigation would be rewarding.

CHAPTER TWO

Setting the Scene

Descriptions of battle situations are gripping, frequently alarming and sometimes even repulsive. This made it difficult for the present author to give an analytical and dispassionate evaluation.

From an evaluation of the specialist literature dealing with the behaviour of soldiers under combat conditions, he had established certain criteria which he used when examining the historical sources for the first time. However, it soon became clear that the pressures were almost always described by the experts in a one-sided and incomplete manner, and that popularly held conceptions concerning combat situations were almost always over-imaginative.

The specialist literature examined is open to criticism because, for example, historians are fond of the word 'panic'. For the purpose of this study panic is defined as: 'Groups of people fleeing aimlessly, running around in circles, shooting or looting, and continuing, either until someone intervenes or until complete physical exhaustion is reached. Crucial in this context is the collective abandonment of all self-control.'

In the battle of Stalingrad documented accounts of panic reactions were to be expected particularly at the moment of the Soviet counter-offensive during the second half of November 1942. This would apply particularly to Romanian troops who had to bear the brunt of the main offensive thrust which led to the rapid collapse of their defence. However, what was described as panic there does not withstand close scrutiny. The sources showed, in the case of the Romanians, that their troops were equipped most inadequately, in a hopeless position, and that from the start they did not intend to resist enemy attack with much enthusiasm. Their retreat was preplanned, although the German Allies were not informed of this. It did not constitute a panic reaction, even if to an outsider it may have appeared to do so. No case of panic, according to the definition, could be found.

The term panic is often found too in the psychological and sociological specialist literature. Thus Marshall[1] describes several cases. They are not based on personal experience and the accounts remain incomplete in his book. (Of course, this aspect is not his main object.) What he does describe, however, allows one to conclude that in these cases, too, we are not dealing with collective abandonment of self-control. The considered actions of individuals were followed by other soldiers who had their own good reasons for doing so. These are examples rather of lack of information or of leadership errors which led to uncertainty and mistakes by subordinates and other troops in the vicinity. Actual panic reactions as defined above are extremely rare. Even this is an important finding.

Nevertheless literary sources deal fairly often with the theme and this is understandable. What is puzzling is why it attracts so spectacularly the attention of all leaders and fires the imagination of nearly everybody. Several of these works on panic are brief and clear.[2] Little can be added. Therefore, we may, for the purpose of this study, disregard panic. There are other, more important subjects. It is much more fruitful to consider what could be termed, by a twist of the original definition, the 'panic of the individual'. Many sources describe again and again a kind of 'desperado behaviour' by individual soldiers, who suddenly lose their heads completely and exhibit suicidal tendencies. Hence it is preferable to attempt an explanation of this hitherto neglected phenomenon, which occurs much more frequently than panic.

In the literature descriptions were repeatedly found of the 'lonely fighter', who has been left to resist the enemy all on his own. He too could not be discovered in personal accounts. A soldier is not easily separated from his friends and comrades. Even if army units break up and retreat in a disorderly manner or flee, old comrades will try to remain together. This explains why units assembled quickly in an emergency under a strong commander could fight with considerable success − a finding which is surprising in this context, as literature tends to claim the opposite.

No doubt it is true to say that in the twentieth century soldiers no longer fight side by side, by going into battle in a shoulder to shoulder formation. Instead, and much to the surprise of the layman, the field of battle often appears deserted. There are no masses of troops or equipment.

Also it may happen that individual soldiers of a teeth-arm unit temporarily take cover alone in a vehicle, bunker or crater. However, a soldier on a battlefield is still not completely isolated, provided he has sufficient strength left to pursue his desire to return to his own small group or to remain with a friend. This is provided that his commander allows him to do so. A soldier who for a while has no visual contact with others may be helped by calling out to them. It comforts him to know that his comrades are not far away, that his commander will not 'ditch' him and that he will be able to restore visual contact as soon as circumstances allow.

However, loneliness does exist. But it is that kind of spiritual loneliness we all have to live with, although it can become particularly acute under the extreme pressures of battle. On the other hand, because of these same pressures, feelings of comradeship and friendship may also be enhanced. So the search for the 'lonely fighter' was abandoned without success.

On the basis of the literature an attempt was made to demonstrate that combat units with losses of 50% will become non-operational. However, many examples were found where losses of 60% and 70%, or even higher, did not lead to collapse. It would appear that the extent of the losses is not necessarily the determining factor in the process leading to resignation or surrender.

The author tried to confirm statements made in the literature regarding the duration of an operation. However, living conditions during a battle differ from those experienced during scientific experiments. A soldier in the field rarely goes without sleep altogether. He cannot be switched on and off like a machine. He gets his rest, which need not necessarily be sleep, wherever and whenever he can. Moreover, the effect of extreme forms of 'stress' on physical fatigue cannot be simulated. Hence on this matter it is possible only to determine trends.

In the literature concerning pressures on soldiers in battle no statements are to be found regarding stress and its effect on the body. This is because findings in this area are too recent. However, it is precisely this new understanding of the mechanism of stress which allows us to comprehend many reactions of soldiers under extreme battle conditions. In the following chapters this subject in particular is studied.

Finally, the literature does not choose to dwell on the fact that soldiers are frequently subjected to coercion of the most brutal kind. Coercion is of far greater significance than Western Europeans like to admit.

This may suffice to show that in the course of examining the sources several new starts had to be made, due to a shifting of aim.

It was also the intention of the author to limit the study to the pressures on soldiers in battle, disregarding all peripheral subjects. In the course of the study it became clear, however, that it was necessary to impart a small number of general explanations. They are as follows:

To begin with we have to clarify the aim of war and combat. Some much-quoted words by Clausewitz describe war as 'a continuation of politics by other means'. An economist might say that 'war or combat have the purpose of destroying an enemy with a minimum expenditure of resources'. Neither of these definitions helps very much here, because this book does not describe whole nations but only individuals or small groups. We cannot disregard these attempts at a definition, and there is no reason for contradicting them, but it is the combatant himself who is most important for our purpose. Therefore, it might be better to use the following definition: 'War or combat have the purpose of forcing an adversary to submit to one's own will'. Clausewitz saw it this way too, but his statements to this effect are quoted less frequently.

It becomes clear now that it is a question of achieving a psychological aim. It is true that important material support is required, but the spiritual and psychological conflict, which already existed before the outbreak of war, does not end when the first shot is fired. In fact, it increases. War means forcing one's own will on others by physical means. Its purpose, however, is not the killing of the enemy. He has to be made to believe that he is weaker and, later, that he is defeated, in order to make him surrender. The dead and the injured are only a means to this end. At its core, war is a battle of minds.

Next, we have to realize what direct effects war or combat have on the individual soldier or the small group.

Our imagination is fired by books and films and we are surprised when we realize that war does not consist only of impressive battles. Even such well-known battles as Stalingrad or Cassino required the soldier to fight only occasionally.

In this age of mass armies and the mobilization of whole nations with resultant long fronts and support routes measured in hundreds or even thousands of kilometres, the average soldier is more likely to encounter a daily routine consisting of loading ammunition, building shelters and polishing shoes, rather than active combat.

Even during operations in the front line, periods of inactivity will prevail. Particularly in modern warfare it is true to say that: 'For half of his life the soldier waits in vain'. Only in a few places and rarely at that, will all efforts be concentrated, resulting in intensive combat activity which puts a company, a battalion or a brigade under pressure to the very limit.

There are many soldiers who, in spite of many years of service during wartime, have never experienced such combat personally, and there are many who have never come face to face with the enemy and who have never attacked him with their own weapons. Therefore, statements or advice given by participants which are based only on personal, and thereby frequently limited experience, are often one-sided. They should not be accepted without question as being generally true. We have to rid ourselves of the idea that in this age of mass armies, soldiers will be in constant direct combat with the enemy.

Nonetheless, intensive combat activity is just as important for this study as it is for other books and films. It is the extreme situation which allows quicker and easier evaluation than the daily routine of the average soldier. At this time the adversaries concentrate all their efforts to decide the outcome of the battle. It is here that the heroic or cowardly conduct of the soldier in the front-line decides the fate of those soldiers who are less involved in the fighting, or who are away from the front-line.

This study, too, reinforces the old truth, which many peace-time armies prefer to forget, that chaos reigns during intensive combat. Chaos, because nearly all the assessments of the situation are based on insufficient information, which a commander under severe pressures will in many cases misinterpret. Chaos, because most of the planning will have little bearing on reality for the same reasons, and because most of the orders issued by higher headquarters cannot, as a result, be carried out wholly or even in part. Chaos most of all, because chance plays a greater role here than anywhere else in life. The combatant needs 'soldier's luck' and his commander, long before Frederick the Great even, has always needed 'fortune'.

If war and combat are psychological conflicts, and if chaos and chance play a determining role, then it can be understood, as the sources too all report, that a battle is won or lost at the lowest level: at the level of the captain and below.

Majdalany, himself a veteran of Cassino, expresses this fact clearly. 'There is no difference between the great offensive and the small groups of men fighting other small groups until one or the other can fight no more' (Quotation 162). Therefore, we have to concentrate in particular on this level.

Majdalany's statement also reveals that there can be no significant difference at this level between small and large scale combat, i.e. between engagements and battles. The source material would appear to confirm this. The behaviour of soldiers who fought for four days for Calais and that of troops who struggled for six months for the possession of Stalingrad or Cassino shows little difference when examined superficially. More thorough examination soon reveals that a soldier is able to fight for a longer period of time than the soldiers did at Calais. But it can be seen also that for most there exists a quite definite upper limit of pressures. This subject is dealt with in chapter 10.

Soldiers of different nationalities react almost always in a similar manner. The British like to see themselves as full of humour, the Poles show their blazing national pride, the Germans emphasize the import-ance of discipline, the New Zealanders like to be individualists, and the Russians show ruthlessness more openly than others. But these are nuances, fixed national characteristics, which affect basic motiv-ation in a marginal way only.

In practically identical situations there is, however, a confusing variety of different and, at first sight, totally dissimilar reactions. This apparent dissimilarity characterizes all ranks, nations and theatres of war. Only when a number of cases sufficient for statistical evalu-ation are examined do we discover the similarities. The apparent differences are merely parts of a jigsaw puzzle. Again, the historical sources do not make it easy for the reader to see the similarities. Hardly any work succeeds in describing the two parties of a conflict without prejudice, which, from a psychologist's point of view, is easy enough to understand. Even historians are influenced by ideology (right or wrong), emotions (sympathetic or hostile) and cultural prejudice such as contempt for any form of coercion.

There are people who seek out danger and deliberately expose themselves to particular risks, deriving a stimulus from this. They are people who consider this a particular challenge and who are proud of being able to stand up to the demands made upon them. There are also people who experience fear to such a minor degree, even during a very dangerous mission, that they hardly notice it at all. The level of fear can vary greatly. It depends for instance on intelligence, training, experience, integration in the group, or the amount of time available before a mission.

Nonetheless, there is a significant similarity between soldiers of all ranks and nations. During intensive, continuous combat in the front line everybody will experience fear eventually. Fear is the common bond.

There are several types of fear which have different degrees of influence. They may even cancel each other out or overlap. Thus fear of mutilation is greater than fear of death. Of particular importance is the physical condition of each soldier. Sleep, food and drink influence fear in a significant way.

As fear is the most significant common denominator for all soldiers and because physical condition is such an influential factor, it is necessary to deal with these subjects at length in later chapters. To begin with, it is necessary to describe a link between body and mind, a biochemical process which we call 'stress'.

NOTES

1. S. L. A. Marshall, *Men against Fire*, p. 156.
2. E. Dinter, *Führungslehre − Arbeitsmaximen und Arbeitstechniken für die Praxis.*

CHAPTER THREE

Stress

There are a great many things which adversely affect the soldier in battle. If he does not eat regularly, his general fitness will quickly suffer. If he does not sleep sufficiently, his powers of concentration will diminish. If he gets too wet, he may catch a cold. These facts will be realized by the soldier only gradually, and they will not begin to worry him until his general condition has deteriorated considerably. If these or similar circumstances begin to worry him, then, in the context of this study, he is suffering from stress.

There are several different definitions of stress. For the purpose of this book it is preferable to select a definition and description which allows an analytical distinction between minor annoyances such as a short-term lack of food, which nevertheless need to be given serious attention, and major, life-threatening factors, which may give rise to considerable fear.

Therefore, in this study the term 'stress' is used only if the physical or mental survival of an individual is at stake. Such a threat may be real or merely imagined. Reaction to it is involuntary. Even noise may be experienced as threatening. We always feel threatened when we are being physically attacked. The 'mid' brain (diencephalon) regulates the adrenal glands via the hypothalamus and the pituitary gland, which release the stress hormones adrenaline and noradrenaline and other adrenal hormones, in particular cortisol. This stimulates blood pressure and circulation and thereby the metabolic process, which improves in a dramatic way the individual's chances of survival. Suddenly, significant physical resources become available, which allow him to fight or flee, thus making survival possible. Stress stimulates and can be a positive factor.

We are dealing here with a reaction which our ancestors learned many millions of years ago and passed on to us. We have very little influence over it. However, our environment has changed. Fight or flight, in a physical sense, rarely takes place in the twentieth century.

Even if they do occur, weapons have changed so much in the meantime that our reaction to stress has become rather a hindrance. This has to be explained in a little more detail.

The first significant realization concerns the feeling of being threatened. The stress mechanism is activated the moment we are threatened directly, for example if someone shakes a fist at us or actually hits us. We often hit back quickly, and regret later that we were unable to restrain ourselves. If someone threatens us with weapons which did not exist millions of years ago, our reaction is either much slower, or does not exist. If, for instance, someone aims a rifle at us from a distance of 300 metres, we do not feel particularly at risk. Our reasoning powers have to interpret the situation before we respond.

Of course, our reaction will be quicker if we have already experienced a similar threat; if we have been hit, or almost hit, once before. Among other things, this distinguishes the experienced from the inexperienced soldier. The situation becomes even more difficult with weapons whose effects we can hardly feel or imagine. In this way, our reaction to an odourless chemical weapon or to atomic radiation may be extremely slow. Our stress reaction hardly helps us at all, because we do not feel in danger. If experiences with such weapons do occur, as in the case of gases during World War I, then our limited capacity for understanding the processes involved will lead to a profound fear of the unknown, very much in the same way as our ancestors reacted to a thunderstorm. This can give rise to stress reactions, which may lead to extremely illogical actions. This subject is dealt with later.

The second important realization concerns the effect of stress on our powers of perception. We all know of situations in life where under stress we reacted in an unbalanced manner. The best replies to make in a quarrel do not occur to us until afterwards, when we have retired and calmed down. Reacting to stress means concentrating on what was important for the survival of our ancestors. A stress reaction filters out everything else. We, as it were, wear blinkers. In such a situation we are perfectly able to hit an adversary with our fists, but we do not see that a second attacker is about to approach from the side, or that the radio we have used for calling up fire support was not switched on. Stress greatly enhances our capacity for physical combat against another individual or for flight and reduces our ability to perceive and think as clearly as we would normally.

A third realization can be reached directly from this. It is of surprising significance for our study that secretions released under stress can be broken down in the body almost exclusively by physical activity alone. There appear to be a few exceptions to this which cannot as yet be explained. This realization is nothing new. It is at the core of many suggestions concerning the ability to deal with stress in civilian life.

Anxieties which an employee may experience every day in the office in the course of his demanding work, and which may bring about a stress reaction, can hardly be translated into physical activity. We are familiar with people who jump up and down excitedly or run around, and we know how beneficial physical exercise is for the office worker. But all things considered, such an employee is unable to translate his anxieties into physical attack or flight. His blood circulation is stimulated but he cannot take advantage of this. On the contrary, he has to suppress the effects as much as possible, so that a possible advantage becomes a liability.

Such an extreme situation can arise for the soldier too, who, so we would think, would actually need his physical abilities during combat. The extreme is created, for instance, when accurate enemy fire causes a soldier's anxieties to reach a peak and forces him at the same time to remain immobile under cover. Also, in most cases, he is unable to release his tensions by other means, such as firing at the enemy at random. The desire to move may become so overwhelming that he might even leave his shelter, in spite of all better judgement, and rush in 'panic' towards his death.

Finally, an acceleration of the metabolic process is part of our reaction to stress. This leads to earlier than normal exhaustion. Drink, food and sleep are required in proportionally larger amounts.

On the basis of these realizations we can now turn to an examination of all the pressures, and in particular the anxieties caused by stress reactions as defined in this chapter.

CHAPTER FOUR

Pressures on the Individual

It has been pointed out already that the subjects of the following six chapters overlap considerably. Hence it does not really matter under which heading the individual aspect is dealt with as long as it is not forgotten and repetition is avoided.

We start with a study of the individual, as in this age of mass armies almost every apparently able-bodied citizen may be called up in time of war. That is to say, almost everybody may have to do active service.

Such service may take many different forms. It may consist of any duty ranging from loading work at a rear depot to close combat in the front line. It is important to realize that what is required of actual front line combatants has increased, since the *levée en masse* of the French Revolution, in a manner never expected or known before. As long as nationalistic feelings prevail, a significant decrease cannot be expected.

It has been pointed out that this front-line soldier decides the outcome of engagements and battles and therefore of wars. Marshall gives a notable example of this in the context of the Allied landings in Normandy on 6 June 1944.[1] He calculates that the success of the invading American forces depended in actual fact on approximately 500 infantrymen in the front line. A few combatants decide by their actions the fate of entire armies, but when they are questioned it becomes apparent that these men are not aware of the significant role they played.

This can be appreciated from studying the examples in the appendices. The question now arises whether this situation will remain unchanged as technology continues to advance. This can be discovered by examining the essential behavioural characteristics of a combatant. He is in danger of mutilation or death, but in spite of this he does not succumb to the will of the enemy. He does not submit. He even retaliates by using his own weapons.

Advances in technology will certainly not decrease weapon effectiveness. The danger to the soldier will become greater and greater. Therefore, even in the future, retaliation will remain an act of willpower. Thus for the individual soldier very little changes. The essential abilities required remain the same. This will be discussed later.

War holds unimaginable, almost indescribable horrors for the combatant. They are so terrible that sometimes death may seem like a release. The work of the soldier cannot be compared with the tasks of the professions. It certainly cannot be compared with the situation of the conscientious objector. The question arises how a human being is able to bear such pressures. An answer may be obtained by examining his anxieties.

All persons involved in combat suffer from anxieties. The level differs significantly for each individual, even in similar circumstances. Many factors influence it. Basically, we should all like to run away. Few, in fact, do so and it is difficult, in the first instance, to understand why.

By using specific examples the thoughts of soldiers before battle can be considered.

A Lieutenant Neave sensed 'danger' while waiting at Calais harbour for his orders (Quotation 9). A Sergeant Petrov was 'scared to death' when ordered into Stalingrad (Quotation 60). The most gripping account appears in two books by Majdalany,[2] a veteran of the battle of Monte Cassino. Referring to experienced soldiers he writes: 'Nevertheless one always experienced a feeling of slight sickness when it [the order to attack] did arrive' (Quotation 98). Later on he reports: 'The ones who had survived many actions wondered how long their luck could hold ...' (Quotation 99).

Other examples can be taken from combat situations where similar anxieties are expressed.

In Calais, injured soldiers refused to be taken to hospital (Quotation 25). At Stalingrad, soldiers in a hopeless situation refused to surrender, because they did not trust the Russians and did not want to become prisoners of war (Quotation 73). The books on Cassino describe how fear increases in foggy conditions or when it is dark (Quotation 103), and the complete disorientation following unexpected enemy attacks from the rear (Quotation 106).

All this is an expression of the 'fear of the unknown and the unexpected'. We are all familiar with these fears, even in civilian life
albeit in much minor forms. Remember the feeling one has when
starting a new job in unfamiliar surroundings, or when at night one
has to walk through a dark wood. A soldier is much more affected
by such fears than a civilian, since it is his own life which is at risk.
Basically, the soldier fears the same things as the civilian, but he sees
them in a much crueller light. He is full of worries. He would like
to know what fate has in store for him. He feels helpless and lonely.
He asks himself many questions such as:

> What kind of demands will my next mission make on me?
> Shall I succeed?
> Will I be mutilated or killed?
> Where is the enemy?
> Where is my nearest colleague, ally or friend?
> Where is my corporal, sergeant, lieutenant, company com-
> mander?
> Will I lose all my comrades, if I have to go into hospital? Am
> I 'written off' in that case?
> How will the enemy treat me if I become a prisoner of war? Will
> I be murdered? Will I be tortured to death slowly? Will he give
> me anything to eat and drink?

The more time the soldier has to ask himself such questions, the
more questions he will find. But hardly anybody will be able to give
him all the answers. Knowledge could be helpful. Majdalany writes:
'Operational existence is much easier to tolerate when you have a
clear-cut objective' (Quotation 112). Rynkiewicz notes: 'We were
dying to know exactly what was happening up on Hill 593 ...'
(Quotation 115). However, such information is a drop in the ocean,
a rather pleasant distraction. It does not explain very much and
therefore the actual fear for life and limb remains unchanged.

Any activity helps to distract and therefore is preferable to the
torture of waiting, as is the mission itself.

Experience seems to help to control this fear for a while, but there
are too many examples where seasoned units did not fight to the limit
of their ability any longer − perhaps because they realized only too
well what lay in store for them.[3] Drugs and alcohol seem to help.
The Soviets gave alcohol to their soldiers before an attack during
World War II and such measures have a long tradition. British

regiments at Waterloo fought in a square formation with a barrel of whisky at the centre. But alcohol alleviates anxiety only temporarily. Moreover, it reduces the increasingly important ability to act in a rational, coordinated manner.

There is only one reliable solution: the individual soldier must live with his own anxieties and learn how to cope with them. Information, experience, drugs and alcohol can improve his situation only marginally. However, there are positive ways of helping him. These are discussed later.

An examination of the historical sources described under the heading 'Pressures on the Individual' reveals many examples − apart from those concerned with fear of the unknown and the unexpected − of two entirely different behavioural patterns for soldiers during combat: whereas one soldier will engage the enemy actively the other will do nothing to resist.

At Calais, the retreat of tank crews into 'shell holes near the Gare Maritime' in order to sleep was ascribed to complete exhaustion (Quotation 34) and the 'game of hide and seek' of platoon commander Stevens was described as 'a remarkable feat' (Quotation 45). Reports from Stalingrad are more candid when describing soldiers sitting on their beds and staring into space (Quotation 77) and when mentioning those who would dare to leave their hiding-places only to steal food (Quotation 78). Most revealing of all are some accounts of Monte Cassino. Majdalany speaks of lazy commanders (Quotation 122) and Rynkiewicz describes the passivity of some soldiers on several occasions (Quotations 120 and 123). In these cases at least, the reasons for such inactivity cannot be ascribed to complete exhaustion as the engagement had up to that point lasted only a few hours.

Marshall's examinations help further. He notes, for instance: 'The thing is simply this, that out of an average one hundred men along the line of fire during the period of an encounter, only fifteen men on the average would take any part with their weapons'.[4] He points out that this figure does not change with increasing experience and that it is always the same soldiers who will fight. This is a sobering thought. Only one sixth to one fifth of the infantry deployed by the Americans in various theatres of war engaged in active combat. At Calais, Stalingrad or Cassino the other nations probably fared not much better. Thus there are fighters, who are like 'drivers', and there are others, who are like 'passengers'. Not that these 'passengers' give up more quickly and run away — there are no signs of that — but they do not participate actively as a driving force or with a weapon, in combat.

Marshall recommends a change in the training and in the delegation of responsibility, so that those with little initiative of their own will still become effective combatants. The success of such a measure remains uncertain, however. Activity or passivity are a matter of inheritance, the influence of background and of education. Characteristics which exist as a result of inheritance or the environment are almost unchangeable, and the process of education is virtually complete by the time a young man is called up. Fundamental changes are therefore no longer possible. Marshall's recommendation is only useful in so far as it may serve to uncover hidden talents.

Much better is his suggestion to integrate the inactive soldiers in groups such as gun crews, where their shortcomings will have no ill effects. Therefore, the answer to this problem can be found in a careful selection of personnel.

But the infantry cannot be allowed to requisition all of the few active personalities (15–20% of the population?) for its own use. Firstly, they constitute the reservoir from which future leaders are drawn. Secondly, in modern war with its shifting engagement patterns, sudden break-throughs, airborne invasions, and fifth columns, it is essential that support services too are able to withstand an attack.

Combat units, too, can use a considerable number of passive soldiers for team duties and a 'passenger' can be a help merely by his presence. The introductory remarks about the nature of combat should be remembered. It is a psychological conflict in which even a man who does not shoot, but simply stays put, can be a factor.

In consequence, there has to be purposeful selection and mix of personnel when filling posts in units either at the front or in the rear. This should take into account, according to their military importance, not only intelligence and other talents, but also personality traits.

This chapter affords two insights. First, the omnipresent fear of the unknown and the unexpected becomes apparent and this results in the desire to flee. Second, two basic types of soldier are defined. They differ from each other not necessarily by their courage, but most definitely by their behaviour. There is the 'driver' who uses his weapon and takes the initiative and there is the 'passenger' who remains passively at his side.

In the next chapter this examination of anxieties is continued. They comprise fears which we have already mentioned, namely those of mutilation and death.

NOTES

1. S.L.A. Marshall, *Men Against Fire*, p. 71.
2. F. Majdalany, *The Monastery* and *Cassino*.
3. See for example S.A. Stouffer, *The American Soldier*, vol. 2, Chapter 1.
4. S.L.A. Marshall, *Men against Fire*, p. 57.

CHAPTER FIVE

Injury and Death

At first sight, statements made by soldiers on the subject of death seem contradictory. On the one hand, death affects the survivors very little, even if casualties on both sides have been heavy. Appalling as this may seem, it is explained by the 'anonymous' almost 'scientific' methods of killing (Quotation 130) or by the nearly incomprehensible large death toll (Quotation 131). On the other hand, there are many examples of the death of individuals having tragic and painful effects on whole groups (Quotation 131).

As happens so often, the paradox is resolved by examining the extremes. The brutal statements made by the riflemen at Calais, who refer to killing as 'glorified rabbit shooting' come to mind as an example (Quotation 19). As a result of the laws of war, these soldiers may, indeed must, violate the generally accepted conventions on killing. Society not only allows the soldier to kill, it indeed orders him to do so. His conscience, which according to Freud 'is in its origin the fear of breaking the rules of society, and nothing else',[1] is thus cleared.

These soldiers were not only without a sense of guilt, but even showed a very obvious pleasure in killing. This seems to be more frightening to us than anything else. Does this mean that laws against killing actually signify the repression of an instinct? Freud postulates this when he writes:

> The pleasure of aggression and destruction belongs in the realm of instincts. The death-wish becomes a destruction-wish by being directed, with the help of particular organs, against the outside world or specific objects. The living being preserves its own life, as it were, by destroying other life.

Referring to primitive man, who he sees reappearing in a soldier in combat, he remarks elsewhere:

He ... was certainly a most passionate being, more cruel and dangerous than other animals. He liked killing and killed as a matter of course. Thus killing is pleasurable ... and closer to our nature than our objection to it.[2]

Civilization rejects this. It seems logical, but we do not like it at all. The author, too, did not wish to accept it without question and endeavoured to find proof one way or another. War veterans were interviewed, but their answers did not provide a basis for statistical evaluation.

In *The American Soldier*[3] reliable statements on the subject were found. Unfortunately they confirmed Freud's thesis. The form in which the question was put did not attempt to overcome sociological barriers. Even so, a remarkably high percentage of the soldiers interviewed stated, even before their first enemy engagement, that they would love to kill a Japanese (44%) or a German (6%). A still higher percentage thought it their duty to kill the former (32%) or the latter (52%). A mere 18% and 34% respectively had some scruples regarding these enemies, and only 4% and 6% respectively had any total aversion. Considering the usual lowering of social inhibitions on the battlefield, interviews on the spot would probably result in statements which could confirm Freud even more emphatically.

The average person does not particularly worry about killing. Such 'fear' is an ancient myth and it can be removed from the list of possible anxieties. Deep down in his subconscious, man seems to enjoy killing.

Now it is possible to understand the reaction of the Calais riflemen, and the reason why the many anonymous dead on the battlefield do not affect the survivors to any great extent.

Why then are they so grief-stricken when a friend, an old comrade, or someone well known to them dies? Here, the answer is more difficult, if one attempts to base it on statistics. The psychoanalytical literature, however, offers a plausible argument, namely that of the feeling of guilt which everyone experiences, because of their enjoyment of killing.

Freud gives the following explanation: 'These dear ones are, on the one hand, an innermost possession of ours, a part of our own self, yet on the other hand also partly strangers and even enemies'.[4] Those who are without pity for their enemies, as well as strangers on their own side, mourn for their friends because part of their own self has been killed. Even in the most difficult circumstances they want to bury their dead with due ceremony because they feel guilty, not merely because they loved them, but also because they were hostile to them. Funeral rites are designed to mollify the dead person, and serve as a method of atonement. The burial of an enemy, however, is by comparison of much less importance. But there is no need to dwell further on the subject in the context of this study.

If killing others is not experienced as particularly worrying, what can be said about the fear of one's own death? Does the death of a stranger or, particularly, the death of a comrade not give pause for reflection, does it not increase the fear of one's own demise?

To answer this question, it is necessary to look again at soldiers in situations in which they had to risk their lives. At Cassino, Rynkiewicz deplores the fact that many soldiers took 'unnecessary risks' (Quotation 120) and in Calais, dispatch-riders were seen charging along the streets full of 'youthful high spirits' in order to ascertain whether they were in range of enemy fire (Quotation 20). The soldiers under Rynkiewicz appeared to act under compulsion, the dispatch-riders acted deliberately. Compulsive forms of behaviour will be examined further in chapter 7. For the moment, it is necessary only to take a look at the high-spirited dispatch-riders.

A point is reached where the available statistics and their method of collection do not or can no longer tally completely with the findings of the psychologists. It is necessary to risk interpreting them. The few existing statistics are equivocal. They deal with fear, but do not investigate the various facets of fear, probably because this is impossible in such a context. Even so, the conclusions are significant:
  — They confirm that everybody experiences fear.
  — They show that fear increases in proportion to the duration of the engagement and the number of frightening incidents.
  — Fear in younger and unmarried soldiers is only marginally less than in older, married ones.
  — Junior officers and non-commissioned officers show a little less fear than the other ranks.

Stouffer[5] concludes that a lower level of intelligence and lack of education are related to a higher level of general fear. The statistics quoted by Stouffer also indicate that fear is greatest when the soldier is forced to remain immobile. This will be dealt with in chapter 7.

However, this chapter is concerned not with fear in general but only with the fear of one's own death. Psychology again provides the answer. It would appear that deep down in his subconscious man does not believe in his own death and is convinced of his immortality. Freud has this to say on the subject: 'Fear of death, which affects us more frequently than we realize, is something secondary by comparison and evolved from feelings of guilt in most cases'.[6] Several modern psychologists speak of 'repression'. This scientific dispute is beyond the terms of this study. In both cases man seems to fear death only when his intelligence, given the time and the opportunity, points out the danger, or when feelings of guilt become too strong. This explains the youthful daring of the dispatch-riders and the more considered behaviour of the older soldiers at Calais.

In that case, if fear of his own death is not so dominant, which fears haunt the soldier mostly? Corporal Matthies from Stalingrad, who runs away from the tanks which are crushing his comrades, gives an indication of where to look (Quotation 66). Even more revealing is the disproportionately strong psychological effect of the bayonet (Quotation 130), or the Moroccan soldiers at Cassino who mutilated their victims (Quotation 134), and who were therefore particularly feared by the defending German soldiers. We are deeply afraid of losing our physical integrity by being mutilated. This fear is so great that mutilation even after death still scares us. Fear of mutilation is certainly greater than the fear of death itself.

We are afraid particularly of going blind or of losing our sexuality. We are terrified by the thought of suffocating. Whereas the sight of a dead person will hardly move the experienced soldier, the burnt corpse of a napalm victim, for instance, will affect him. The many false gas alarms in Calais are an example of this fear (Quotation 14).

Injuries which do not lead to mutilation do not frighten the soldier so much. Many continue fighting in spite of their injuries (Quotations 23, 25 and 65). Many envy these injured soldiers, because they have a genuinely acceptable reason for withdrawing from the fight (Quotation 133) and some will even inflict injuries upon themselves in order to enjoy similar rights.

What are the main findings of this chapter? They are frightening. First, we know that there is no definite abhorrence to killing. A time-honoured prejudice is destroyed. There are many indications that killing an enemy can even be a pleasure.

Second, the fear for one's own life does not seem to be as great as has been assumed. A second prejudice is destroyed. Other fears are stronger in any case. Third, there is a strong fear of mutilation, whereas minor injuries are almost welcomed.

It can now be understood that the unknown and the unexpected scare soldiers a great deal, that the possibility of being mutilated terrifies but that, on the contrary, threats to his own life and the possibility of minor injuries are accepted with comparative equanimity.

The following chapter examines the reasons behind the capacity for stamina. In this way, the study more or less corresponds to the order of the historical quotations, and later embarks on the search for possible additional fears.

NOTES

1. S. Freud, *Zeitgemässes über Krieg und Tod*, p. 321.
2. S. Freud, ibid., p. 357.
3. S. A. Stouffer, *The American Soldier*, Vol. 2, p. 34.
4. S. Freud, op. cit., p. 344.
5. S. A. Stouffer, op. cit., Vol. 2, pp. 81-6 and 446.
6. S. Freud, op. cit., p. 342.

CHAPTER SIX

Stamina and Exhaustion

As before, an insight into the factors governing stamina and exhaustion in soldiers can be gained only by studying intensive combat situations. Emphasis is placed on a small number of war veterans in situations which occur infrequently, and on companies and battalions of combat troops engaged in a prolonged, uninterrupted battle. Units further to the rear and higher headquarters must be disregarded for the purpose of this study.

The theatres of war selected supply sufficient examples. In Calais, the defending troops appear to have been completely exhausted after four days (Quotations 29 and 31), whereas in Stalingrad they were still resisting enemy propaganda after five months (Quotations 73 and 75). At Cassino, the German paratroopers fought on with determination, even after 220 days of continuous combat, and the American 34th Division defended their positions with such dogged resolve that many soldiers had to be carried out when relieved (Quotation 139).

Endurance for four days or for 220 days, the ability to walk back after the battle or the inability to move at all due to exhaustion, seem to be the extremes. Of course, for the purpose of this study such a finding is insufficient. Further details are required regarding the meaning of endurance and, in particular, a differentiation is necessary between the factors which finally lead to exhaustion.

W. Noyce deals with the subject and examines a number of individual cases.[1] He analyses the behaviour of a miner buried underground, of trapped polar explorers, of shipwrecked sailors, of lost mountaineers, of a hermit and of a cancer patient, all of whom willed their bodies to superhuman efforts. This cannot be applied directly to military situations, because more than mere survival is involved. In addition the soldier is supposed to take part in active combat. Moreover, the behaviour of individual personalities cannot be applied to large armies. Nevertheless, Noyce's book provides some answers.

The first is that there are some people who will fight instinctively for survival. They might even say occasionally that they do not care any more about their survival, but unconsciously they still clutch at any straw, even if others next to them have long since given up.

The second is that it is practically impossible under normal circumstances to distinguish these people from those with less will-power. Criteria which reveal the ability for physical endurance are not relevant here.

The third is that these people possess already, or develop, together with their unconscious will to live, a deep faith in not being alone. They are, or become — in the widest sense — religious.

The fourth is that nearly all maintain a friendly relationship with others.

The final answer is that most of these people have a sense of humour, at least one of self-irony.

Thus we have a number of partial answers, but for the first time in this study it is not possible to make a categorical statement. All one knows is that many human beings are able to endure unimaginable sufferings. They may be completely exhausted after a few hours, yet they can carry on living under constantly bad conditions for days, weeks or even months. The limits cannot be defined precisely. At the other end of the scale, it is possible to identify those factors which lead to rapid exhaustion.

All soldiers complain about tiredness, thirst, hunger, noise, heat or cold. In the history books and the historical sources, we often find unintended hints of this. For example the German soldiers in Stalingrad complained at the height of the fighting that their own air superiority was coming to an end. Russian bombardments were increasing even during the night, making it impossible for them to sleep. This surprises those without battle experience, because they do not expect soldiers to sleep at all in such a situation.

Sleep is important. Everybody has experienced how lack of sleep can affect the ability to react. There have been numerous scientific experiments on this. Their results are unambiguous, but additional factors such as thirst, hunger, noise, heat and cold, as well as fear, were largely ignored.

If young people are deprived of sleep completely, their efficiency is reduced after 24 hours, after 48 hours it is severely restricted and after 72 hours it is non-existent. If the experiment is continued, hallucinations will soon set in.

It would be more realistic to assume that a soldier will find the time for at least a few hours of rest during 24 hours. The result is then very different. Given a mere four hours of sleep per cycle of 24 hours, a control group can remain operational for a longer period (9-14 days), even though their efficiency will be very much reduced.

According to the statistics available, four hours of sleep seems to represent the time available to most soldiers in the field. However, towards the end of the Italian campaign, one third of the American soldiers examined had to make do with less than four hours of sleep each night, and 85% with less than six hours.[2]

Stimulants of all kinds, from coffee to specially manufactured drugs, can of course temporarily increase the ability to make do with little or no sleep over extended periods. In view of the increasing night-fighting capability of modern weapon systems this is not without significance.

Those documents which are openly available lead to the assumption that the taking of psycho-stimulants or amphetamines may set free considerable physical reserves. If their use is controlled, there would seem to be no significant subsequent damage. However, their disadvantage is that reserves once called upon always need to be built up again later. Sleep not enjoyed at one time must be recouped without fail at a later stage. In this way, these stimulants merely buy time. They cannot solve the problem, but, indeed, complicate it further.

Articles which have appeared in magazines seem to indicate that the Soviets are carrying out meaningful experiments in this field. It may not be without significance that papers on this topic have been absent recently. If for ethical or pragmatic reasons we ourselves do not undertake any research in this direction, we should at least pay careful attention to the activities of other nations.

When studying reports on sleep deprivation, one always has to bear in mind that, in normal circumstances, the groups examined would sleep 7-8 out of 24 hours. Moreover, this would be at regular intervals in keeping with bodily rhythms (biorhythm). Any variation of this pattern leads to a reduction in efficiency.

It is also important to realize that the ability of the body to make do with less sleep cannot be improved simply by training. One can merely learn how to reduce the negative effects of sleep deprivation by organizational measures. For instance, as the number of errors increases, control must be stepped up.

It is possible to manage without sleep altogether for approximately two to three days, and to remain operational, but only just, for nine to fourteen days with approximately 4 hours sleep each 24 hours. However, these are the absolute lower limits, which presuppose a very much reduced efficiency. If other factors such as heat or cold occur during combat, greater allowance has to be made for sleeping time.

Soldiers also complain about hunger and thirst. Statistics confirm these complaints.[3] A soldier under combat stress requires, like someone with a fever, more liquids than a person not under any stress. Due to the many variables in this area, it is not possible to give figures, but one should accept that beverages should be distributed at least once a day.

We know that a man can survive for some time without food. The problems of hunger are vividly described by patients forced to go temporarily without food for medical reasons. Even the cancellation of one habitual meal can affect the ability to concentrate as well as reduce physical energy. In the confusion of combat one sometimes forgets to eat and, as a result, exhaustion is much greater later on.

If food can be supplied only in reduced amounts, the physical efficiency of the soldier will decline rapidly and he will soon become listless. Greater physical efforts, such as those required during an attack, can no longer be expected, although he may still just be capable of static defence.

Rapid exhaustion due to additional noise, as well as heat or cold, has to be mentioned only because it is forgotten in peacetime in pleasant surroundings, and quite often overlooked by leaders in war. The 5th American Army deployed in the front at Cassino may serve as an example. They had more casualties due to frostbite and colds than to enemy action.

Finally, stress accelerates all those bodily functions important for survival, and thus speeds up the metabolic process. It has been pointed out already that this accelerates exhaustion, which in turn leads to an increase particularly in the amount of liquids required. Sleep requirements and appetite are also affected, although not to the same extent.

The importance that must be attached to satisfying such basic requirements as sleep, food and drink is shown clearly by some of the following examples:

In Stalingrad, Captain Muench allowed the mutineers in his battalion to sleep, eat and drink. Following this, he had no difficulty in persuading them to continue fighting (Quotation 93).

In Cassino, Major-General Baade recognized the importance of good and regular food supplies, and, even as a divisional commander, organized this himself (Quotation 145).

Major-General Oster, who served as a major at the Cassino front, remembers the amazing success which Major-General Baade achieved with his field-kitchens in holding together his division, which had started to give way gradually under extremely heavy enemy fire: Baade assembled his soldiers about 3 kilometres back from the main fighting-line at several field-kitchens, gave them food and drink, assigned positions to them in the vicinity and allowed them to rest. After approximately 2 hours he was able to send them back to the front-line and to their old positions from which they had run away. No coercion was required.[4]

Fulfilling the basic human requirements of sleep and food is just as important as the right tactical decision and the deployment of effective weapons and reliable equipment.

The account concerning Major-General Baade would not be complete, without mentioning another of his many unconventional measures. This concerned 'hope'.

In all accounts of the stamina of soldiers or civilians, hope plays a decisive part. One can carry on just a little longer, bear just a little bit more, if one knows that the end is in sight.

The most impressive example of the importance of hope is an evaluation of the German postal censorship in Stalingrad, which reflects the erosion of hope as the situation worsened (Quotation 63).

Major-General Baade understood this very well and pressed for long-term, firm planning of leave and relief, which would be altered only in the utmost emergency. Everyone knew about this and therefore had an attainable goal to aim at (Quotation 146).

The American Forces in Vietnam applied this principle to all their soldiers, who were relieved annually. This seems to be one of the main reasons for the above-average decrease in the number of psychiatric casualties, compared with the Second World War.

If a man loses hope, he is tempted to commit suicide. This was probably one of the decisive motives for the large number of suicides among soldiers in hopeless situations.

Hopelessness can have exactly the opposite effect, however, particularly on those few active personality types described in chapter 4. If the aggression resulting from hopelessness is not directed against oneself in the form of suicide, it can lead to an increased, even fanatical will to fight. As there is no alternative, as there is 'nothing to lose', the enemy is attacked with fury. However, this reaction is exceptional because in hopeless situations vitality is often so diminished, due to lack of food and sleep, that only a few remain capable of such physical effort.

As significant as hope, and to a certain extent comparable with it, is religious faith. Interest in religion increases during times of crisis as everybody knows from experience. There is a revealing account from Cassino by Major-General Oster[5] concerning this. He explains that the paratroop divisions under the command of the Luftwaffe were much more influenced by Nazi ideology than the average German army division. Because of this the paratroopers had no chaplains. They suffered terribly at Cassino, and in their distress secretly 'borrowed' chaplains from other army divisons.

The statistics in *The American Soldier* reflect the same experience.[6] They show an increase in religious conviction for 80% of the combatants and a decrease for only 20%.

A considerable number of soldiers repress reality, sometimes in the most peculiar way. All of us sometimes make such attempts, even in peacetime. As Freud remarks: 'Illusions appear to us, because they save us from frustrations'.[7]

In Stalingrad, Sergeant Pflüger, who was injured, withdrew into 'daydreaming' (Quotation 65), Corporal Fehrmann made plans to travel, Corporal Michel made clocks (Quotation 64) and even on 31 December a private wrote home that 'our Führer will not leave us in the lurch' (Quotation 74).

Even those illusions, this flight from reality, which can rise to the point of fanaticism, help one to endure. Of course, one's comrades and the group also help. This will be dealt with in chapter 8.

Lieutenant Neave, fighting in Calais, summarizes the first part of this chapter, when during the first day of fighting he notes: 'Fatigue, thirst and the need to do the right thing, made it difficult to think clearly ...' (Quotation 27).

The ability to bear the pressures of battle and the will to endure are greater in man than might be expected. But lack of sleep, drink and food, and factors such as noise, cold or heat and fear will diminish within a matter of hours the ability for positive action.

Majdalany, fighting in Cassino, sums up the second part: 'You endure anything if you know when it is going to end' (Quotation 137). Hope, religious faith, even the various stages of illusion help to keep one going in otherwise intolerable situations.

NOTES

1. W. Noyce, *They Survived*.
2. S. A. Stouffer, *The American Soldier*, Vol. 2, pp. 78-9.
3. S. A. Stouffer, *The American Soldier*, Vol. 2, p. 79.
4. Private discussions with author.
5. Private discussions with author.
6. S. A. Stouffer, *The American Soldier*, Vol. 2, p. 172.
7. S. Freud, *Zeitgemässes über Krieg und Tod*, p. 322.

CHAPTER SEVEN

Firepower

The literature contains many accounts which describe how companies, battalions and even regiments were decimated, or reduced by over 50% through death and injuries within a few hours, by fire from aircraft, artillery, tanks, rifles and machine-guns. The appendices include a number of these descriptions (Quotations, 80, 81 and 150).

Since the end of the Second World War the effective load capability of aircraft has risen steadily. The calibres of artillery and tank weapons are getting larger, the rate of fire and target accuracy of all weapons systems are improving and the effectiveness of single bombs and rounds of ammunition is becoming greater.

Studying the sources, the author encountered very early on the statement: 'The remarkable thing about modern shelling is not how many it kills but how few' (Quotation 147). There seemed to be a paradox. Further study showed very quickly that this contradiction had to be resolved, because evidently, apart from physical injuries and death by artillery fire, a wider most effective psychological influence is exerted. Expressions such as 'baptism of fire' and 'shell shock' indicate this. Therefore, the effectiveness of enemy fire in relation to two components, one physical, the other psychological, has to be examined.

First, the physical aspect. Every gunner knows how difficult it is to hit a target, let alone destroy it. A little applied mathematics allows one to understand this easily. Let us take a very simple model, in which a battalion of 1000 soldiers is distributed evenly over a surface area of 5 square kilometres. They are fired at in a grid pattern, with traditional 155 mm artillery ammunition with a fragmentation area of 50 by 100 metres. In this model 5,000 rounds are required in order to hit every soldier. This is more than the ammunition used by an entire artillery battalion during five 'average' days in combat.

If every one of the 1,000 soldiers digs a foxhole of one square metre, and if it is assumed that only those hits which detonate within an area of 10 square metres around the centre of such a foxhole, will cause injury or death, then the effective fragmentation area of previously 5000 square metres is reduced to 1/500. It would then be necessary to fire 2½ million rounds in order to hit every soldier.

In practice, there is of course no even distribution of soldiers and rounds of ammunition. Moreover, the number of soldiers in the battalion and the size of the fragmentation area have been exaggerated, whereas the effectiveness of cover is rather underestimated. The type of terrain and its very important predominant features (e.g. sand at Calais; snow or rubble at Stalingrad; rock or rubble at Cassino) were not taken into account. Armour and particularly mobility were not considered either.

But one fact is demonstrated very clearly by this simple model. The probability of a soldier being hit by chance in the field is extremely remote. Fire is only effective when carefully directed against a specific target.

What kind of directed fire was used at Stalingrad and Cassino? In both cases, more artillery and aircraft were concentrated than in any other action of World War II. Aircraft could be counted in hundreds, guns in thousands. The greatest concentration of fire was achieved during the preparation for an attack. For twenty minutes, one hour, or even longer, known or assumed enemy positions were bombarded in order to make them ripe for attack. However, no evidence was found that this was ever achieved to a degree even approaching expectations, much to the surprise of friend or foe alike.

Let us recall the 2½ million rounds of our example. If applied to the much larger areas of Stalingrad and Cassino, where soldiers could take cover in bunkers reinforced with concrete, and where any kind of target location was difficult, then it can be appreciated how even 3000 or 7000 guns could have surprisingly little effect on enemy soldiers in an hour. Therefore, artillery men the world over strive for improvements in target acquisition and accuracy. It is the laying of fire, not its amount, which has the decisive physical effect.

For the sake of completeness it must be explained how those horrendous losses mentioned in the appendices came about. They occurred when the soldiers had to leave their reinforced shelters during an attack or retreat and then came under direct fire by artillery, tanks and, particularly, small calibre guns. Flanking machine guns operating from covered positions seem to have been the most murderous weapon of all, even in World War II.

Fire also buried and destroyed many weapons held ready for fighting, communication cables and trench systems. This factor is not to be underestimated, although it is in no way as important as injury, death or the anxieties of the soldier.

Even if fire is not accurate it can contribute considerably to confusion (Quotations 37 and 38). Later in this chapter we shall discuss stress reactions due to fire. Suffice it to say at this point that dust or accurately laid smoke may increase the already existing chaos during an engagement, because they eliminate the visual contact which is indispensable to any form of coordinated action (Quotation 160). Moreover, the fear of the unknown, as described in chapter 4, increases considerably.

Experience is a major factor where fear is concerned. The soldier who comes under fire for the first time is considerably frightened (Quotation 33). This 'baptism of fire' raises his anxieties to a level seldom reached again. If he is able to control them under such tension, he will probably be able to endure more stress situations.

Therefore, experienced soldiers say that the baptism of fire separates 'the men from the boys'. Those who are psychologically weak may crack up even as early as this.

As was noted in chapter 4, frightening experiences do not toughen up a person. They have a cumulative effect, and thus a psychologically strong person will gain experience during this baptism, but his resistance has of course already sustained some initial damage.

The experience gained relates particularly to an estimation of the effects of fire. An experienced soldier is often capable of judging by the noise made by the projectile, whether or not a round will land close to him. Also he learns how to judge the effects of a hit, and he is not unduly worried by a hit 200 metres away, even if it kills or injures his comrades (Quotation 35). If he reckons, however, that fire is approaching his direction, as was the case with rocket launchers or during bombardments during World War II, or if a round is a near-miss, then his anxieties increase dramatically.

This has probably to do with man's inherited flight-or-fight reactions as described in chapter 3. An intimidating threat, such as a fist of an adversary punching at one's face, is more disquieting and leads to a quicker reaction than a rifle aiming from a distance. In the first case we react instinctively, in the second only because of our experience and intelligence.

The psychological and physical effects of fire depend on its accuracy. The near-miss is very worrying, a hit some hundreds of metres away is comparatively less disturbing, at least for the experienced soldier.

Concern about a near-miss is increased when it is not apparent where the threat lies. The feeling that the enemy is able to observe and attack freely from a hill or a tower (Quotation 161), or that he is in the rear and attacking from unknown positions, causes extreme stress (Quotations 104, 105 and 106). The fear of the unknown starts to grow. The snipers of Calais (Quotation 12), the sharp-shooters in Stalingrad, and the bombardment of the unoccupied monastery of Cassino are clear examples.

Noise plays a part (Quotations 33, 36, 148 and 149). Even under normal peacetime conditions, noise is a strain or stress, ranging from irritation to pain. Hence, weapon systems which create above-average noise, like fighter aircraft such as *Stukas*, and multiple rocket launchers such as *Nebelwerfer* and *Stalinorgel*, will worry the soldier more than other systems when they score near misses.

Statistics in *The American Soldier* prove for instance that the inexperienced soldier is more afraid of enemy aircraft than of enemy artillery. After 5 to 10 days his attitude changes completely. Both weapon systems are now seen in the context of their effects. Artillery is now considered to be twice as worrying as aircraft.[1]

Finally, a long period of fire, such as preparation for an attack, forces the soldier to remain still. He has to stay under cover, and cannot move for longer periods of time. He feels that his existence is threatened. (Will the next bombardment hit me?) The noise is unbearable. Dust and heat make breathing difficult. An acceleration of the metabolic process causes persistent thirst. Immobility gives him time to think. (How long shall I be able to bear this?) His comrades are being injured or killed. Perhaps he might be buried. He can do nothing. The paratroopers in Cassino are an example of this (Quotations 148 and 149).

Such a situation comprises all the aspects of the physical and psychological effects of fire, which are maximized by the fact that no one is able to move. In such a situation fear is at its greatest.[2]

The stress mechanism is activated, but the soldier has no opportunity to make use of the additional physical capacity created thereby. He can neither fight nor run away. He cannot even move. He is 'stressed' to breaking point, like a car, when the driver after engaging the clutch, steps on the accelerator with one foot, while braking with all his might with the other. If such stress is sustained long enough, one force or the other will win. The car either shoots forward or the engine stalls.

The same happens with the stressed soldier. At some point his situation becomes unbearable. He runs, against his better judgement, or attacks with apparent heroism (Quotations 28 and 123) and is killed by the continuing enemy fire. He commits a kind of suicide which is completely different, however, from all the other forms of suicide, because it is the result of prolonged, enforced immobility.

This suppression of the ability to move is also described as a feeling of hatred against the enemy. The terrible example of Petrov who experiences a traumatic Volga crossing and then butchers everybody in sight is an example (Quotation 60). Here, too, it is primarily the chemical process in the body, rather than emotion or rational thinking which compels the soldier. Hatred plays a much less important role than is often assumed, certainly as far as the experienced soldier is concerned.[3]

Finally, every soldier who is forced to become immobile will experience the filtering out of the stress reaction in a particularly strong way. It reduces him in an atavistic manner to a level of processes which were important for survival in prehistoric times. He loses all sense of time (Quotations 116 and 117) and he is practically incapable of clear thinking or operating complicated equipment (Quotation 140). What was once helpful has become a disadvantage for the twentieth century combatant. A high level of stress is often followed by heavy, general exhaustion which may lead to apathy.

Many soldiers are thrown aside by the blast of the explosions (Quotation 153). They lose consciousness for a time or are so dazed that they can no longer act in a reasonable controlled manner. Or they are afflicted with a kind of paralysis. This is discussed in chapter 11. The findings of this chapter are important not only for airmen and gunners. Only fire which hits or almost hits the enemy has a significant effect. If such fire is sustained over a period, the resulting immobility may lead to irrational reactions in the soldier. This applies especially if he does not know how to reduce his tension by physical activity. Even in the most confined spaces he should at least shout or shoot, if necessary without a target. In order to put a soldier under this kind of pressure, the shelling has to continue for long enough. ('Long enough' meaning perhaps 30 minutes but more likely one hour. The parameters are unknown.)

Only hits and near-misses will lead to the required result. The creeping barrage of fire advocated in Soviet manuals on military tactics is largely a waste of ammunition.

All soldiers under fire have to 'let off steam', even if this, like shouting perhaps, or shooting without a target, does not comply with standard military behaviour or is against regulations.

NOTES

1. S.A. Stouffer, *The American Soldier*, Vol. 2, p. 236.
2. S.A. Stouffer, ibid., p. 82.
3. S.A. Stouffer, ibid., p. 158.

CHAPTER EIGHT

Experiences of Military Units

In 1940, the British government sent four formations of battalion strength, including a high percentage of reservists, with undue haste across the Channel to defend Calais. The soldiers fought bravely until injury, death or lack of ammunition made a continuation of the fight impossible (Quotations 40, 43 and 45).

The battle of Stalingrad, because of its size and duration, is more revealing. The combat units of the 22 German divisions fought as honourably as their British opposite numbers at Calais, even when the situation became more and more hopeless (Quotations 83 and 84). Most of the Romanians succumbed within a matter of hours to the Soviet counter-offensive, which began at the end of November. On 12 January, German support units withdrew from the vital airport of Pitomnik because of a single enemy tank (Quotation 86). On 26 January, a Romanian regiment of 1100 men deserted to the Soviet side (Quotation 87). Finally, German army officers openly accused their own Air Force of deserting them (Quotation 89).

Notable examples at Cassino were: the American 34th Division, whose men fought until exhausted and unable to walk (Quotation 139); the German paratroopers who in spite of appalling losses did not surrender the town of Cassino (Quotation 150); the New Zealanders, who were brought into action because it was believed that they would succeed in carrying out the apparently impossible task of breaching the German lines (Quotations 164 and 166); the Poles with their dogged determination to attack (Quotation 169).

The question which arises is why some units fought better than others in similar circumstances. The answer which appears in several specialist publications is usually given as 'group integration'. As there is unanimity, it is necessary only to deal briefly with this subject in order to give a complete picture of the pressures on soldiers in war-time.

Furthermore (and here the present study differs from the other literature), the additional attachment of the soldier to the people back home, the particular effects of strong group integration on other groups and of female soldiers, will be discussed subsequently. This has organizational and even socio-political consequences explained later on. But first, the combat unit, the small group.

The book *The American Soldier* contains a survey of the main reasons for stamina in combat.

Almost 40 per cent of those questioned simply wanted to fulfil their task and get the fight over and done with. 14 per cent mentioned the small group. No other reason was given with any similar frequency.[1] With less specific control questions, e.g. those concerning attitudes to dishonourable discharge from the armed forces,[2] or pride in one's own unit,[3] the percentage of answers indicating a strong group integration rose to 80 per cent. This is a very high figure if one also takes into account the 'don't knows', but the answers merely confirm what is already known.

The small group comes into being because it has to perform a task which cannot be carried out by a single person. (This may be a subjective feeling or an actual fact.) Therefore, initially, the group is determined by expediency.

However, apart from wanting to perform his task, each member of the group is interested in satisfying his own personal interest. In this way the expedient group becomes a social group from the very moment it is assembled. The strongest emotional force in this socially constituted group is the desire of each of its members for love, friendship, sympathy, recognition, respect and power. In this context these requirements are synonymous. As the group of soldiers exists under extreme pressures, because it has to complete an almost impossible task, while the individual is tortured by all sorts of anxieties, the process of satisfying his needs is much more important than in any civilian group, because it must compensate for the hardships. Hence social relationships within the small combat unit are incomparably more intensive, and after returning to civilian life many members recall them with nostalgia.

The group also offers the individual shelter from the hardships of his surroundings. Together, it is easier to protect oneself from them than alone. The need of the small combat unit for self-preservation is particularly strong, as is the interest shown by its members in the group.

Although these groups undergo constant internal structural changes, due to the different strength and nature of the members' personal interests, each individual (on whom the group as a whole depends for completion of its task) is given a certain protection against the other individual members. Food, for instance, is handed out in a fair way – according to the group's definition of 'fair'. A group structures its inner workings by a network of regulations.

If the members are rather weak and passive, they like the network to be as comprehensive as possible. If they are very self-confident and are dynamic, they do not consider this to be quite so important. The number of regulations is still surprisingly large, because even a strong personality has a definite desire for protection.

Finally, the group may be able to help the individual to realize his ambitions. It can make promotion and income-earning easier. However, these motivations are less important to front-line soldiers than they are to civilians.

In an environment which is both physically and psychologically threatening, the group understandably gains a significance of otherwise unknown proportions for the individual. Without it, he could not survive either physically or psychologically. Hence each member of the group has two vital interests:

Under no circumstances does he want to be rejected by his group. That would be the end for him. There is nothing he fears more. Therefore, he continually strives to prove his usefulness to the other members of the group, and to the unit as a whole. For a small group in active combat this usefulness means the ability to fight, and so a member of a strongly coherent group will participate actively in battle.

However, this individual is still beset by fears which actually make him afraid of fighting. He is afraid of the unknown, of the unexpected and of mutilation. The group is able to take some of his fears away by its protection. But it can do even more for him. It gives him love, friendship, sympathy, recognition, respect and power. The fear of losing these helps him to control those other fears which the group has already reduced. In this way, fear helps to exorcise fear and fire is fought with fire. That is the reason why a member of a group, in comparison to a lonely individual, is able not just to fight, but to do so with courage and devotion.

Apart from wishing to continue to remain a member of the group, each individual has a very strong interest in preserving the group as a whole. He realizes that the group is in the greatest danger of breaking up when integration into other groups would be easy, because these groups have a very similar structure. Each member understands intuitively that it is necessary to be different from the other groups.

This can be achieved successfully by such simple devices as uniforms and insignia. It is also possible for it to be different because of its reputation and not because of special personnel or weapons. That is the reason why special 'elite' units often fight better than those without a special image. Preserving one's own reputation preserves the group. It is possible to show a group's individuality by rituals and customs. Acceptance into the group may depend on special conditions such as a parachute jump. Members may have to take oaths, there may be special initiation or expulsion ceremonies. These things are often laughed at, but they are most important to instil the individual's confidence in his group.

Abolishing such differences would only lead to a loss of confidence among the established groups.

Close relationships within the group can continue to exist and grow only if the relevant primary group is small enough for close social interaction between members. Strong and increasing cohesion, depending on the duration and the intensity of togetherness, can be observed only in tank crews, platoons and perhaps small companies. The ideal group has no more than 3-5 members because such a very small group can be commanded and controlled more easily in the chaos of combat.

Taking into account other additional factors, military organizations tend to favour larger rather than smaller groups. This need not be a significant disadvantage, provided that the primary group is no larger than about ten.

It is obvious that group cohesion remains effective only if the group has sufficient opportunity to establish and further its relationships. This requires time and a challenge. If the members change constantly owing to a particular system of replacement, or because a military situation requires it, it will take a certain amount of time before the social structure of the group has recovered to the point where it is possible to speak again in terms of a bond. Up to that point, the operational value of the group and its individual members remains low. Marshall's statistics confirm this.[4]

The process of integration in newly formed groups can be speeded up by giving the members certain options. A member may choose the group he wishes to join, he may select another member, the leader may decide upon his subordinates and, in some situations, they may choose him. Thus everyone shares in the responsibility for himself and the others, and from the start strong social bonds are established.

In times of war the challenge which encourages group cohesion can be found easily. In peacetime, however, it has to be created with care. It may be a taxing training exercise or 'adventure training', which is perhaps even better, because it is different from everyday routine.

Incidentally, it should be pointed out here that our upbringing has conditioned us to believe that all tasks should have a good reason and that even in difficult situations fairness should be observed. Observing these postulates has its advantages and it is not recommended that they be abandoned. This does not mean, however, that armed forces which do not always follow these criteria are to be considered inferior as far as group cohesion and therefore operational efficiency are concerned. Even occasional senseless tasks and unfairness, suffered together, can weld a group. Problems will arise only when certain limits are not observed. Then the group's ambition may change, for instance from fighting the enemy to fighting its leader.

Strong group cohesion often leads to the elimination of members who plainly do not help the group or harm it. Mere inefficiency is treated with indulgence. A group will protect its 'idiot'. But particularly at risk are those who establish or maintain connections which are likely to cause actual harm. Members with strong relationships with other groups, or with particularly intense relationships with one another thus setting themselves apart, and members who fall in love, are examples. In such cases, the group often resorts to expulsion, which is cloaked in rituals and traditions designed to scare other potential sinners.

This leads to the problem of integrating women into groups, such as small combat units under operational conditions, when it might come under extreme pressures. Cases are known where the integrated women assumed an unusual role, such as that of her male counterpart or that of the 'slave'. However, as soon as it became a matter of equal participation, based on employing the natural abilities of group members of either sex without prejudice, love relationships came into being. Due to their totally different structure (intensive one-to-one relationships without much interest in the social environment) they began to undermine group cohesion. The men in question no longer fought for the group, but for their much stronger relationship with their girlfriend. This led to irregularities and severe offences against group morality, when the loved one seemed in particular danger of being injured or killed.

As such relationships cannot be avoided, and in fact, are encouraged by close living conditions within the group, the inclusion of women in small combat units will destroy group cohesion and thus reduce its operational value. If women must be allowed into the armed forces, then they should be organized as a separate unit. If that is not possible they must not, under any circumstances, be assigned to small combat groups which might come under severe pressures.

The intensive cohesion and differentiated morality of a group derive from a strong 'inward centration'. Groups are 'self-centred' and as a result, the importance of the environment decreases.

This begins with the flow of information. The members of the group are interested only in information which is directly useful to them. What is happening in the neighbourhood is less important and higher headquarters is far beyond their horizon. Thus information has to be virtually squeezed out of these groups. Frequently they do not even know the name of their brigadier.

Hence the enemy is much less hated than is generally assumed.[5] Hatred as a motivation is not very significant, although the statements concerning the Poles at Cassino (Quotation 168) might indicate otherwise.

The enemy who differs strongly from one's own pattern because of his race, appearance, behaviour or culture or who is merely reputed to be different, will be despised and thus often underestimated. This serves as a self-protection against other groups which are considered to be strong.

If the enemy shows considerable professionalism, it is not possible to hate him any longer. On the contrary, he is respected to a degree, almost like an opponent in a sporting event. Feelings of hatred and revenge are the results of fleeting frustrations. If for instance a good friend has just been killed, these emotions increase, but as time passes, they diminish rapidly again. The average soldier does not maintain constant feelings of hatred and revenge. Any training in this respect, as carried out in some of the Warsaw Pact countries, is of almost no consequence under operational conditions, and is a waste of time.

Just as the enemy, in spite of being a threat, is incapable of arousing overwhelming emotions, so is the neighbouring brigade, another arm or service, or one's allies. If feelings are aroused at all, then these are usually negative because of the soldier's concentration on his own group.

There are many examples in the historical sources which show that allies may be despised just as much as the enemy (Quotations 1, 5, 11, 87, 88 and 89). *The American Soldier* confirms this. In August 1945, the French Allies had a worse image than the recent German enemy.[6]

The more an ally differs from oneself by appearance, language or manner, the more he is distrusted. Nobody should have any illusions about the feelings which exist between Warsaw Pact countries or between NATO Allies.

For the same reasons there are no indications that soldiers fight for a political system such as democracy or for their own government (Quotations 100 and 171). The historical sources confirm this clearly.

As neither the soldier nor the civilian population are able to discuss this question unemotionally, it might be helpful to quote some reliable statistics from the USA, whose understanding of democracy is rarely put in doubt. In *The American Soldier* only 5% of those interviewed stated that they were fighting for ideological reasons. This meagre percentage includes those who were motivated by patriotism or a burning desire to reform the world.[7] Many soldiers in battle (32%) do not even believe that they are fighting in a conflict that makes sense, and a further 56% believe this only occasionally.[8]

Political indoctrination is no more helpful than trying to further hatred. The successful person does not need it and the failure is not helped by it. Other things are more important to him. In this field, too, the Warsaw Pact is a victim of its own ideology.

Nonetheless, the definition and publication of a general motive for defence should not be neglected completely. It affects the willingness to enlist and it is important to the attitude of the people back home towards the soldier in the field.

There is also no proof of soldiers fighting less well in a foreign country. The British in Calais, the Germans in Stalingrad, the soldiers in the battle for Cassino demonstrated this over and over again.

The much-published story that the Soviet Union became successful after many defeats in the Second World War, when it changed its general motivation from a demand for a fight to defend the socialist system to a call to defend the fatherland, is nothing but a fabrication spread by popular journalists and historians.

In order to avoid misunderstandings it must be pointed out here that the defence of one's own country can constitute an additional motivation. But this does not depend on ideological or political beliefs. It depends on the importance of the people back home to the soldier. This is discussed later.

Thus, the 'self-centred' attitude of the group has a number of significant consequences, not all of which have been mentioned.

For instance, the influence of a continuous retreat. Hitler was of the opinion that any form of retreat would destroy combat morale (Quotation 71). The German paratroopers at Cassino proved the reverse to be true. Thus the 'self-centred' approach of the group leads to the belief that one is fighting better than the enemy, or that one has the better weapons. Such a belief is a double-edged sword. It is helpful, if it is not too far removed from reality. But if it is, it will lead directly to disaster.

The effects of strong group cohesion on attitudes to the equality of the sexes, to allies of all kinds and to political values are acknowledged only reluctantly and most ungraciously accepted by many soldiers and civilians. They cannot, however, be ignored. Even if the 'self-interest' of troops could be reduced or eliminated, this would not mean that a very personal interest in sexual equality, in allies or in democracy could be aroused. Every soldier (as indeed most people, even when not particularly under pressure) would during combat desperately seek to attach himself to a group. However, a group whose cohesion had been deliberately weakened would not be able to help him to control his fears and fight with courage. Deprived of his strongest support, the soldier would hardly be able to muster the necessary will to resist required for active fighting, and would surrender or flee. Thus, dependence on the group is either strong or weak, and there cannot be a middle ground. A weakness in the integration of the group leads directly to defeat. It is again time to abandon some previously held beliefs.

Having established the primary importance of group cohesion with all its consequences, the question arises whether the examples of

Calais or Stalingrad where units were thrown together quickly might contradict the findings (Quotations 57, 58 and 85). The answer was suggested earlier. The average soldier cannot be separated easily from his comrades. Those units that were thrown together and fought successfully consisted chiefly of many well-established small groups. There may have been the odd strong-minded individual less influenced by the factor of group cohesion than the majority, but average soldiers fought only when group cohesion remained intact. Marshall's research confirms this fully.[9]

If group cohesion is so significant for the combat value of a group, then it may be used also as a basis for an evaluation of the importance of discipline. Formal discipline, like parading and drill, is of no consequence to the ability of the group to deal with the demands of active combat. Thus troops who, like the New Zealanders, gave the impression of being particularly relaxed (Quotations 163, 164 and 165) were by no means less successful than those who, like the German paratroopers, maintained a very formal image.

Combat drill helps in mastering the more technical tasks. Even under the pressures of combat it is an advantage to operate weapons quickly and reliably and to perform minor tactical tasks faultlessly. Furthermore, the ability to carry out routine duties amidst the chaos of combat inspires a feeling of order which strengthens the self-confidence of the individual.

Some of the measures which superiors impose for reasons of discipline correspond to those which everyone's self-discipline would require anyhow, if they wish to establish some form of comforting order. Majdalany for example describes his personal method of hygiene (Quotation 110).

A most important form of self-discipline is humour. Everyone can release tension for a few minutes by laughter. He can relax and take a deep breath, not unlike a diver who is caught by a giant squid yet manages to surface for a moment (Quotations 17 and 109).

This kind of humour is not just a gift, it can be acquired. This requires extra strength. Therefore, humour can often be seen in conjunction with a light-hearted recklessness. The dispatch-riders in Calais (Quotation 19) and the bets of the two soldiers in Stalingrad (Quotation 82) are examples.

But even purely formal discipline such as shoe-shining, which has no purpose, may become a way of strongly distinguishing the group, and thus expresses group cohesion. This effect is often overlooked and therefore underestimated. As far as combat morale is concerned, it is mainly a question of reinforcing the 'centration' of the group. If group cohesion is very strong, then the desire to be different is not so pronounced, but it is still latent. Hence it is not very sensible to try and suppress harmless forms of self-assertion by formal discipline. It would be just as unreasonable to ban an outward show of relaxed behaviour. This may get the same results as formal behaviour. In any case, efforts to change this or that are misguided in that they miss the actual target, the creation of group cohesion. Quite often they actually endanger it.

The integration of the individual in the group is so strong sometimes that the group's destruction, e.g. by force or captivity, may lead to depression and subsequent suicide (Quotations 69 and 70).

In such cases it is often impossible to determine whether the fear of the unknown played an important role too. However, it is surprising that a considerable number of soldiers commit suicide immediately after being deprived of their duties within the group (Quotations 90 and 91).

So far we have only talked about the small combat group. It is, indeed, the primary group for the soldier and has the greatest significance for him. Beyond that every human being is also a member of many other groups, which in this study will be called secondary groups. In this way, the soldier does not only belong to the small combat unit, but to his company, his battalion, his brigade, his division and his arm or service. The link with these groups becomes more tenuous as their size and anonymity increase.

A combatant does not belong only to military groups. Civilian groups also retain their significance. Among these, the most important is his family and friends back home.

All soldiers mention the importance of letters from home (Quotation 62). This dependence becomes even more apparent in the case of the mutiny in Captain Muench's battalion in Stalingrad (Quotation 93) and in the behaviour of the New Zealanders (Quotation 166). Most soldiers depend on their girlfriends, wives, parents, children and friends. Keeping in touch with them, in addition to being part of the primary group, is a second life-line. Ten per cent of those interviewed in *The American Soldier* mention this secondary group when asked about their most decisive motivation for fighting.[10]

The opinion and the behaviour of the general public back home is also of some influence. The soldier wants everybody to recognize his effort and to assist him as much as possible.[11]

But most dominant are intensive love relationships. Wives or girlfriends attain a significance they never had before. In the field they are often idealized and this may lead to problems of readjustment on coming home. But it is also a question of self-esteem. A soldier does not fight so well if those for whom he cares most do not give him recognition as well as love.

Any force which loses this moral support will find its combat efficiency reduced. If the group cohesion remains intact efficiency will not be destroyed completely. Thus integration of armed forces with society and the common identification with the aims of the war are not the dominant factor. However, through the link of the soldier with his family and friends, they are of considerable importance.

So far, the major anxieties of the soldier have been analysed. This chapter has taken us a decisive step forward. It is now known that the soldier's fear of losing both his primary group and the love and recognition of the people back home, exceeds his strong fears of the unknown, the unexpected and mutilation. The conclusions which must be drawn, as far as the organization of armed forces is concerned, are obvious. The consequences for society are unavoidable.

It is clear also that strong group cohesion can be a great and often unique experience in life. Nonetheless, we should never forget that the average soldier would really like to run away from the fighting. The group prevents him from doing this. If group morality allows for an 'honourable' means of flight, it will be accepted gratefully.

At Calais, soldiers destroyed their tanks prematurely, allegedly because of a misunderstanding (Quotation 10). They used up their ammunition as quickly as possible (Quotation 11). At Cassino they were glad to be injured (Quotation 133), and they showed unconcealed joy upon being relieved (Quotation 126). All this reflects the constant conflict between fear, group cohesion and morality.

The influence of leaders on these factors is investigated in the next chapter.

NOTES

1. S. A. Stouffer, *The American Soldier*, Vol. 2, p. 108.
2. ibid., Vol. 2, p. 115.
3. ibid., Vol. 2, p. 138.
4. S. L. A. Marshall, *Men against Fire*.
5. S. A. Stouffer, *The American Soldier*, Vol. 2, p. 158.
6. ibid., Vol. 2, p. 566.
7. ibid., Vol. 2, p. 109.
8. ibid., Vol. 2, p. 152.
9. S. L. A. Marshall, *Men against Fire*.
10. S. A. Stouffer, *The American Soldier*, Vol. 2, p. 108.
11. ibid., Vol. 2, pp. 319-321.

CHAPTER NINE

Experiences of Commanders

In chapter 4 active and inactive personalities were discussed. These characteristics also apply to the leader. Freud writes: 'It is a part of the inherited and unchangeable inequality of men that they are divided into leaders and followers. The latter constitutes the vast majority, they need an authority, which makes decisions for them and to which they submit unquestioningly in most cases'.[1]

The quotations contain examples of leaders chosen by the military organization and holding a high rank in the hierarchy who did not provide real leadership. These cases are intended to show that conferment of leadership responsibility and formal authority by rank does not necessarily create a leadership function in the Freudian sense, and that total exhaustion may result in leaders also becoming inactive.

In Calais, for example, a colonel shirks his responsibilities at the port installations of the Gare Maritime (Quotation 46). At Stalingrad, the Chief of the General Staff of the *II. Armeekorps* is exhausted after long fighting and gives up (Quotation 92).

It is evident that leadership requires more than conferment of responsibility and rank, and the leader is subject to at least the same pressures as his subordinates, and he, too, is soon so drained that he is unable to complete his task.

But the quotations also include examples which indicate a strong desire and need for leadership, thus confirming Freud. How else could we explain the fact that so many soldiers obeyed senseless orders at Stalingrad (Quotation 92), and the collapse of his troops after the sudden death of Captain Meus, a man hitherto thought invulnerable? (Quotation 96).

There are subordinates who look for leadership and there must also be someone with leadership qualities – not necessarily dependent on rank. His activity is considered in detail later.

To begin with, let us consider the nature of the influence which the leader has on the performance of a group engaged in completing a task.

It is difficult to answer this quantitatively. Some statistics in *The American Soldier* seem to indicate a minor degree of influence. A mere 1% of the combatants interviewed stated that their leader was the decisive factor in their determination to carry on fighting.[2] The replies concerning the leader show that 'task', 'group' and 'family' are more important. This does not necessarily make his influence insignificant. The importance of this influence has to be considered first.

It was noted in chapter 8 that the military group is formed for the purpose of solving a task, which cannot be carried out by an individual.

There are other incentives leading to group formation which also apply in civilian life. For instance, the group protects its members against external and internal threats, by its strength, its laws and its morality. A strong group, which offers these advantages, will be strongly centred on itself and will set itself apart from outsiders.

The group will consist of a few leaders and many followers. As its leader the group chooses – sometimes consciously, mostly unconsciously – the person best able in the first place to look after the interests of the group as a whole and its individuals.

The group expects several things from its leaders and members. The members of a small, experienced combat group value particularly courage (59%) and ability (28%) in their comrades. They do not place particular emphasis on leadership qualities (8%).

This percentage changes considerably when the question refers to desirable qualities in leaders. Courage remains very important. 42% require it of their corporals and their sergeants, and 30% of their officers. Professional knowledge ranks very much lower. Nineteen per cent expect it of their corporals and sergeant, a mere 13% of their officers. But the desire for leadership ability and experience rises suddenly to 33% for corporals and sergeants and to 56% for officers.[3]

The group thus selects those who show outstanding courage, like Lord Cromwell in Calais (Quotation 59), or the fearless sergeant at Cassino, who carried his wounded subordinates through the firing to safety (Quotation 181). It chooses someone who also shows leadership ability and experience.

The latter is a generalization. We understand the anxieties of Lieutenant Neave in Calais before he proves to be a leader (Quotation 48). What else does a courageous leader have to do in order to gain the esteem of his subordinates in these categories?

The group has to solve a difficult problem, and therefore it has to be convinced of its importance. In Stalingrad, Captain Muench's treatment of his mutineers (Quotation 93), his Christmas speech (Quotation 94) and his reaction to Soviet propaganda are examples.

Although the situation in Calais was apparently hopeless, Carlos de Lambertyne and the officers of the Royal Green Jackets succeeded in recruiting volunteers by convincing them of their cause (Quotations 57 and 58).

Montgomery's briefing of his leaders about future plans for operations was a similar case (Quotation 177). The leadership level is merely higher, and the groups involved are not as coherent as those of the infantry at the front. The 'cabinet' of General Freyberg had the purpose, beyond gathering information, of persuading its members of the necessity of tackling an unpleasant task.

Persuading the group of the importance of its task begins at the lowest level. If it is not successful there, the consequences will be the most serious. But other groups, such as officers of headquarters staff, and groups further to the rear, such as maintenance units, have to be motivated as well. Only when all these groups are taken together do they form a balanced fighting force, and if the various groups cannot be convinced that their cause is worthwhile, soldiers of all ranks may become inactive, or even mutiny, as did the German Navy in 1918. Even entire armies may collapse, as in Russia during the First World War and in France in 1940. Incidentally, this shows how difficult it is to motivate combatants when people at home are not convinced.

A leader with an assured and agreeable manner and the gift of being able to express himself well will have a small advantage. Every leader is in possession of information. In the chaos of battle, information is almost a means of power. The groups take a burning interest in everything that directly affects their future. This is precisely the kind of information that a clever leader will be able to obtain. By passing it on, he will gain influence. His men will listen to him eagerly. If his information proves to be accurate, and if he passes it on without twisting it, then a kind of trust will be created. And this, in turn, allows the leader to exert this influence.

However, all this is rather an intellectual process. Communication of any sort must continue even at the lowest level in frightening combat situations. In Calais, Lieutenant Neave realizes that there is nothing to be done 'except to encourage the ... men as they fired bravely, but inexpertly, towards Boulogne' (Quotation 49). Nicholson 'travelled long distances encouraging the men in the front line' (Quotation 50).

If distance makes direct conversation impossible, for example when a group of attacking riflemen is suddenly forced to take cover in various positions without visual contact, communication must be maintained by shouting at each other. Communication between the leader and his subordinates is so important that it should be maintained at all costs, even if necessary by radio.

Of course, his mere physical presence helps (Quotation 51), particularly when he appears calm and full of confidence (Quotations 52 and 179). He must be with his subordinates, bear the pressures and lead by example. Böhmler explains this vividly in his account of the German paratroopers (Quotation 171).

In an emergency, the leader must not be afraid to make physical contact with his subordinates. Physical contact, such as an embrace, given by a leader to his subordinate, or by a soldier to his comrade, provides the same feeling of security that a mother gives to her child. Existing social conventions should not be an obstacle in such situations.

Trust is the major basis. Words and actions will have an effect on the individual only if a basis of trust exists already. Leaders who do not mean what they say will never achieve that trust, because body language reveals to the subordinate the discrepancy between the spoken word and the actual attitude. This usually happens in an unconscious way, but sometimes consciously. Sometimes play-acting may be successful for a while. However, in the long term it will be recognized for what it is, and will create a feeling of mistrust which may be impossible to remove.

Trust will grow only slowly. The leader and his subordinates have to work, live and solve problems together, until such time as they are attuned to each other. The leader must be able to prove:

- that he will ask his subordinates to do only reasonable things;
- that he is capable of planning and leading with success;
- that each member of the group is important to him;

- that he is looking after each member of the group;
- that he is doing everything to ensure the support of the group from outside;
- that he will 'get out' anyone who is in trouble.

This, then, is what is meant by leadership ability and experience. This is what happens when a leader works for the interest of the individual and is the ideal of the informal leader.

To what extent does the formal leader selected and assigned by the military system approach the ideal described above?

During the Second World War, a surprisingly high number of leaders were capable of approaching this ideal. In the American infantry, for instance, 28% of the junior leaders and 30% of the other ranks stated that they would attempt any task under their officers. A further 38% and 41% respectively believed themselves capable of solving most tasks under their officers. A further 20% and 17% respectively thought they could solve at least every second task that arose. This constituted an outstanding vote of confidence which, however, was not quite so remarkable when compared with other arms and services.[4]

So far we have noted that the leader is basically dependent on the interests of the group and its members. He has means of influence, but just how strong are they? Is he merely capable of increasing existing interests, or can he persuade the group to accept new tasks which it may reject initially?

In the appendices there are several examples of a need for leadership. Under pressure, human beings revert to their basic needs (see Maslow's 'Pyramid of Needs'). This is a form of 'increased infantile behaviour'.

This means that in a stressful situation many people will search for a 'father figure'. The more autocratic this figure appears to be, the more the feeling of protection and security will be reinforced. In such situations the only things that many group members require of their leaders are clear orders and a will to succeed.

Of course, the father figure of the leader becomes even more dominant if in addition to authority he also shows warmth, sincerity, reliability, trustworthiness and a deep concern for the individual. During World War II many German soldiers referred to this as being 'hard with a heart'.

Thus the leader is not only the person best equipped to look after the interests of the group and the individual, but to many he is also an important authority capable of changing things.

The sources contain examples of frightening violence which show leaders apparently transgressing the bounds of their parental role and acting against the interests of the group and the individual. Most depressing are the commander of the Soviet 64th Division, who executed soldiers at random during the collapse of his troops (Quotation 97) and the guards who accompanied the transport of soldiers to Stalingrad (Quotation 60). Given the insight gained so far, we must ask ourselves how such brutalities could succeed.

Majdalany writes: 'You must never acknowledge that abnormality exists. Once you do the whole structure of morale is bound to collapse' (Quotation 107). General Stempel emphasizes this, when he says to his son in Stalingrad: 'Conduct yourself to the very end like an officer and a gentleman' (Quotation 92).

In chapter 8 it was pointed out that, particularly in the chaos of war, rules guaranteeing a certain order and support, and thereby giving stability, must not be abandoned. Those who do not obey the written and unwritten laws of their culture and their group will eventually destroy their self-esteem and pride, and thus their will to live.

If one considers the brutalities mentioned above in that light, then those responsible for them merely enforced existing regulations. Those who had infringed them, either by thoughts or deeds, had to accept punishment as a form of penance if they wished to regain their self-esteem. Therefore, they did not turn against their potential murderers and obeyed orders unquestioningly, even after the atrocities.

Nobody wishes to condone brutality. These extreme examples merely serve to illustrate the fact that a leader must use the full force of this authority to enforce the laws of the group. This is often possible only by means of apparent viciousness and an apparent lack of consideration to others. If he is not tough enough to act in this way, and does nothing, he will damage himself and others, because he is creating complex feelings of guilt. He is undermining the morale of the group.

This insistence on regulations has more compassionate aspects. Only a sadist will seek to increase the fear of the individual on the battlefield. Any psychologically normal person will try to reduce these fears, provided he himself is not too dominated by them. For example, German forces who called local cease-fires to recover casualties made them against the express orders of Hitler. They may also represent some form of enforcement of written or unwritten laws.

Ultimately, leaders like Captain Muench in Stalingrad (Quotations 93 and 94) also exerted pressure when they visited their men to talk to them and to motivate them to continue the fight. This pressure was of a subtle kind and cannot be compared with the measures of the commander of the Soviet 64th Division. But it is pressure, albeit gentle, to remind soldiers in a desperate situation of their duties to the group. Admittedly, it is a kind of pressure which is more readily acceptable to Western Europeans.

If one talks about leadership at the present time, so full of complex tasks and abounding with well-trained soldiers in Europe, one would have to talk also about cooperative methods of leadership and delegation as well as the related responsibilities. On this subject, the literature is almost unanimous in its findings.[5] In this study, all that is important is the fact that these methods of leadership represent a recognized means of achieving motivation. The acceptance of responsibility acts as an incentive.

This leads to the last question to be answered in this chapter. How can a leader muster the additional energy required to assist the group specifically in completing its task, given the fact that he is subject to at least the same physical and psychological pressures as his subordinates?

Parts of this question have been answered already. Accepting the task of leadership and its allied responsibilities acts as an incentive and sets free additional energy. There are specific 'leader-types' and only they may be entrusted with this difficult, extra task. This is discussed further in chapter 13.

Nonetheless, it is probably true to say that in spite of incentive by responsibility and careful selection of personnel, leaders tend to 'burn out' more quickly than their subordinates. Leading is more difficult than being led.

Leaders cannot be successful if they ignore the interests of the group and the individual, are unable to play the role of the father figure, are too soft to enforce the written and unwritten laws of the group, or are exhausted and burnt out. Then there is only one solution which will help both the leader and his subordinates. He must be relieved of duty.

The example of General Baade (Quotation 160) merely represents the tip of the iceberg. Leaders were frequently removed from duty. Some who were highly efficient one day could carry on no longer the next.

Many of these sacked commanders were successfully re-employed after a period of rest. It is not dishonourable to relieve exhausted men, and it is part of the welfare responsibility of every senior officer.

This chapter showed us that the leader is less important than group cohesion or the link with the family, and that he can be successful only if he is in agreement with the aims of the group and the interests of the individual. Frequently, he becomes a father figure with the power to change the course of events by his determination. He must be tough, because he has to enforce the existing laws, even if he should be thought ruthless or brutal.

If he is, and does all these things, his men will go 'through hell' for him. Nonetheless, he is not fully integrated into the group he leads. He is subject to special pressures and he must be studied further.

NOTES

1. S. Freud, *Warum Krieg*, p. 360.
2. S. A. Stouffer, *The American Soldier*, Vol. 2, p. 108.
3. All statistics are taken from S. A. Stouffer, *The American Soldier*, Vol. 2, p. 133.
4. S. A. Stouffer, op. cit., Vol. 2, p. 120.
5. For example E. Dinter, *Führungslehre*.

CHAPTER TEN

Summary of Pressures

In the preceding six chapters the pressures facing soldiers have been described. The battlefield with all its horrors and deprivations cannot be compared with any other situation in life. The soldier is driven to the limits of his physical and psychological endurance.

There are a number of factors affecting men in civilian life which recur on the battlefield, often in an extreme form. These are general deprivations or over-stimulations, such as too much information or too little, too much activity or idleness, too much sex or none at all, too many people or total isolation, too much responsibility or none. The biorhythms are ignored, self-esteem is damaged, isolation is nagging. But there are other factors which affect only particular individuals, such as the specific terror of illness or pain, a fear of snakes or a sensitivity to unpleasant smells.

In addition to these factors which affect everyone in personal and varying ways, there are a number of further dominant factors which come into being during active combat. Again, these affect the individual to differing degrees, but owing to their intensity they do not compare with anything in civilian life. The most important of these factors are illustrated diagrammatically.

These factors resemble a dark, heavy rain-cloud called the 'Cloud of Pressures'. It consists of the primary, all important fear of physical or psychological isolation, the almost equal fear of the unexpected and the unknown, the still considerable fear of mutilation and, finally, of those physical deprivations or over-stimulations already mentioned, among which lack of sleep and noise appear to be the most consequential.

This dark, heavy cloud rains into the 'Lake of Complete Physical and Psychological Exhaustion'. When the lake becomes too full, the water has to find an outlet and will flood the shore. If it stops raining, the water level will fall, but will never evaporate completely. But after a period of drought the lake is capable of holding a considerable amount of rain.

'CLOUD OF PRESSURES' AND
'THE LAKE OF EXHAUSTION'

1. Fear of Physical or Psychological Isolation (Group, People at Home)

2. Fear of the Unexpected and the Unknown

3. Fear of Mutilation

4. Physical Deprivations or Over-Stimulations (Noise, Thirst, Hunger, Heat or Cold, Lack of Sleep)

General Pressures and Individual Anxieties

This part of the diagram illustrates the reaction of the individual to the pressures of war. The lake represents the individual. Fears already existing in civilian life and pressures already suffered during the war have given the lake a personal water-level.

Now the cloud will burst at the moment of the combat situation. Its rain, consisting of additional fears and physical hardships or over-stimulations will come down onto the land and into the lake. The speed of filling it will depend on the heaviness of the rain. That part of the diagram illustrates the way in which the fears and physical influences accumulate as time passes.

If it rains long enough, the lake will fill and eventually overflow. This signifies the point when physical and psychological breakdown occurs. The breakdown, the flooding, is delayed when the rain is not very heavy or when there are periods of drought. This illustrates the importance of the intensity of fighting and of periods of rest.

Finally, the lake can never dry out completely. After long periods of rain, much more water will remain for a longer time than usual, or for ever. The water level is then already higher than usual when a new season of rain begins. This explains the situation of the soldier with combat experience, who goes into battle with a higher anxiety level than the newcomer.

This diagram of the 'Cloud of Pressures' and the 'Lake of Complete Exhaustion' has to be given further thought in relation to the accumulation of pressure factors, which may result in the maximum limit being reached, and the higher anxiety level of experienced soldiers. The next chapter attempts this.

CHAPTER ELEVEN

Psychiatric Casualties

This study was not written for psychologists or psychotherapists and it is not intended to describe such topics as methods of treatment, but rather to concentrate on highlighting points of interest to military leaders.

The extent and significance of the problem must be examined first.

During World War II two million men were discharged early from the United States Armed Forces on various grounds. This included the 389,159 soldiers whom the Army alone had to send home between 1942 and 1945 because of psychiatric problems. Most of them were national service men (375,333).

During 44 days of operations in Italy, the 1st American Armoured Division suffered 250 wounded and an additional 137 psychiatric casualties (54%) in the fight for the 'Gothic positions'. At the same time, the 91st American Division had 2700 wounded and 919 additional psychiatric casualties (30%).

The few figures available for the German Wehrmacht show that smaller numbers were affected.

During the war of 1973, the Israelis suffered (depending on the source used) 10% or 60% psychiatric casualties, based again on the number of wounded.

There are many other similar statistics, but the few examples given allow only two conclusions to be reached.

First, the number of psychiatric casualties in Europe and comparable areas is generally lower than the number of other wounded. Nevertheless, it remains high enough to create a considerable additional problem for commanders and the medical services.

Second, the differences between the figures quoted above are so great that there is a possibility that 'rogue' figures have been entered into the statistics.

First of all it is necessary to define a psychiatric casualty. A most interesting report[1] was submitted to the British Parliament in 1922 when it debated pensions for war victims. The question was whether victims of 'shell shock' should be included. The report concludes, after long and careful consideration of statements made by specialists and sufferers, that there is no such thing as 'shell shock'. Therefore, it suggests that a distinction should be made between three different states.

Concussion occurs relatively rarely. Its immediate consequences are known, although these still cannot be explained completely (Quotation 153 for example).

Total exhaustion is the result of sustained excessive pressure and occurs very frequently. It can lead to behaviour patterns which, at least to the layman, are almost indistinguishable from neuroses.

If generally recognized 'honourable' ways of escaping further pressures exist, as for instance the state of 'shell shock' during World War I, then these routes are all too easily followed. Casualty figures rise abruptly, but drop again if treatment is not delayed, and is given mainly in forward areas. This does not allow soldiers to escape from the danger area and those affected are soon ready to resume duty. In order to be restored, they require only 4 to 12 days' rest and distraction.[2]

Neuroses occur in a relatively small number of cases (10% of the mentally exhausted and 2–3% of all those to be discharged).

They are particularly frequent in inexperienced troops during the first few days of combat. The number of neuroses can be reduced mainly by specific selection of personnel before national service, but also during training and by skilful preparation for combat.

For the reasons already mentioned above, treatment is more successful in these cases, too, if given close to the front line rather than in hospitals far removed from the action. (A remarkable suggestion for a semantic distinction between these three states has been made).[3]

Finally, it is interesting to note that the number of totally exhausted and even the number of neuroses varied from unit to unit, even if they fought in similar conditions.

None of the more recent studies contradicts the conclusions of this 1922 report and even the figures supplied are more or less confirmed.

If the number of concussions and neuroses is relatively small, and if most psychiatric casualties are caused by total exhaustion, then it is necessary to examine the significance of the accumulation of anxieties and the increase in exhaustion in relation to the time spent in combat. As far as the cumulative effects of anxieties are concerned, the statistics show that experienced soldiers rate their own ability higher than do inexperienced soldiers, whereas the will to fight and the ability to endure are rated lower.[4] Even when asked directly whether anxiety increases the more combat is prolonged, a surprisingly high number answered 'yes'. This would seem to be in conflict with the image of the 'old warhorse'.[5]

These statements should be capable of confirmation by the number of casualties. If one compares graphs for injury and death, based on extensive samples, with graphs for total exhaustion and neuroses, one notices at once that they follow parallel courses.

In Europe, casualties due to injury and death were usually higher (at least during the first few weeks in active combat) than those due to exhaustion and neuroses. This may change, if additional pressures occur – if, for example, the group is operating in unfamiliar surroundings or if the period of combat is excessively long. The Americans fighting in the Pacific are an example.

On the whole, however, both graphs rise or fall at the same time. Injury and psychiatric casualties appear to exist in direct relation to each other. This picture changes completely if inexperienced soldiers only are considered. Then, psychiatric casualties are at their highest at the beginning of an operation. Then, as has been mentioned, the chaff is sorted from the wheat. Casualties reach a low between the third and ninth month of operations (less than one third of the initial casualties?), provided that the fighting is not too fierce. Then they rise again.[6] These periods are reduced to weeks if operations require continuous contact with the enemy.

These statistics have to be interpreted with care, as it is not possible to determine how those injured or killed in the meantime would have behaved. (There may be a connection between injury and death and psychological pressures.)

However, this study of casualties, in conjunction with the questions mentioned above, enables a trend to be seen. It is certain that anxieties increase in the course of a military operation. The experienced soldier who has been in combat longer, will therefore suffer more from these anxieties than his less experienced colleague who has been under pressure for a few days only.

Moreover, these anxieties apparently do not disappear again completely, even after a long period of rest. Major Poole (Quotation 56) may serve as an example. In spite of his experience and previously proven ability, he showed 'bad nerves' in Calais. There are other impressive examples from the history of war which show that for the reasons mentioned above, troops experienced in combat often fight less well than troops fighting for the first time. In some cases the veterans' will to fight was so weak that they had to be relieved.

If anxieties accumulate and do not completely disappear, even after longer periods of rest, then there must be a kind of efficiency diagram for soldiers in combat.

Swank and Marchand carried out a study during the Allied landing in Normandy in 1944.[7] This included psychological and physical pressures. They obtained the graph which is reproduced below.

The time axis of this graph is not necessarily definitive. Other similar studies use time periods of 90 to 120 days respectively. The first part of the curve shows that there is a period of adaptation. Then follows a long phase of great efficiency during which anxieties can be controlled fairly well. This is succeeded by an extended phase of exhaustion of which the solider himself is not aware initially. During this phase self-confidence is greater than actual efficiency. The soldier over-estimates his abilities. Finally, he reaches the phase of total exhaustion. For instance, he can no longer distinguish between the various noises on the battlefield. Suddenly, he is no longer capable of evaluating enemy fire and each detonating shell sends him nervously running for cover. He is highly excitable and over reacts to any stimuli. Even minor upsets lead to outbreaks of fury and good news is received with exaggerated elation. If the soldier cannot be relieved when he has reached this state, his excited mood will change to apathy.

There are great variations in the graphs for different individuals. Both researchers are of the opinion that 2% of all soldiers can resist pressures for an almost unlimited period. This would correspond to other findings.[8] The average soldier, however, reaches a point where he cannot go on.

These pressures, previous operations, the duration and the intensity of the current operation, and the individual himself, all help to decide when this point is reached.

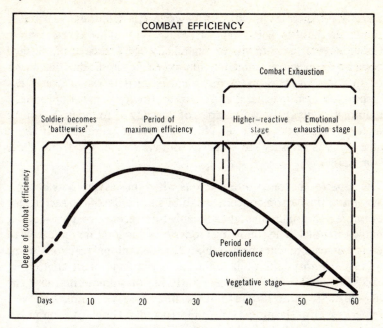

Days in Combat in the Normandy Campaign: portrayal of the relation of stress and the development of combat exhaustion to the combat efficiency (heavy black line) of the average American soldier.

(Swank and Marchand – Combat Neurosis 1946)

Another interesting criterion was found. The moment of reaching breaking point depends also on the nature of the operation. Landings and break-through attempts impose the greatest pressures. Attacking towns is more difficult than attacking positions in rural areas and defence is easier than any attack. On the basis of the findings so far this would appear to be logical. Perhaps this should be taken into account when composing and selecting units for specific tactical tasks.

Taken as a whole, these findings on the accumulation of anxieties and the decline in efficiency should remind all leaders that their subordinates should be relieved at the right time. There are ample warning signs.

Every soldier during, or shortly before, an operation, will show some changes in behaviour. Neither he nor his superior should be alarmed if the symptoms are as follows: dry mouth, rapid heart-beat, ringing in the ears, cold sweat, nervousness, shaking knees or slight trembling, vertigo, a temporary inability to think clearly, diminished powers of concentration, confusion, vomiting, stomach pains, head- or tooth-aches without obvious cause, difficulties in breathing, incontinence, muscle pains and stiffness, tiredness and sleeplessness, nightmares, depression. Examples of this may be found in the source material (Quotations 37, 38, 140, 142, 151, 152 and 154). It is not absolutely necessary to relieve soldiers suffering from these complaints.

The situation becomes more serious when these symptoms become acute and the person concerned exhibits a change of character. For example a careful man might suddenly turn reckless or a great talker may keep quiet. The following modes of behaviour are indicative of great exhaustion: extreme irritability, over-emotional reactions, some loss of memory, fits of laughing or crying, incessant chattering, excessive smoking or drinking, stuttering or stammering, extreme nervousness, paralysis due to shock, unnecessary running for cover, remarks such as 'I can't go on', aimless activity, clinging to comrades, whimpering, shaking limbs. Again, examples can be found in the source material (Quotations 77, 95 and 139). It is advisable to relieve soldiers exhibiting these symptoms.

Relief from duty is inevitable if the soldier becomes disinterested and listless. He may also show loss of memory and become depressed and apathetic. During the transition to neurosis, which can occur at any stage, the soldier may suddenly go blind, deaf or dumb. The sources contain a few examples of timely and organized relief (Quotations 136, 144 and 146).

The above cannot be used as a check list. Transitions from one phase to the next are not strictly defined. They can occur abruptly or gradually. The list is intended as an indication of what may still be called quite 'normal' behaviour. It indicates when, apart from carrying out the many other measures described, relief should take place.

This list can also be used for information. Every soldier should know that he is still fit for combat, even if his heart is racing or if he is vomiting. A part of this information should also affect the attitude of the individual towards his comrades suffering with these symptoms and should be aimed towards influencing this attitude. On the one hand, there must not be an 'honourable' way out for the soldier, such as 'shell shock' during World War I. On the other hand, an understanding of these debilities should be encouraged. The soldier under pressure needs special attention; if he is despised by his comrades or superiors, this may drive him over the edge.

A compromise acceptable to everyone would appear to be the following. Debilities such as crying or trembling are accepted with understanding by those around, but the person concerned must demonstrate to the group his will to continue fighting by clear attempts to control his anxieties. If this is plainly no longer possible, he should be relieved at once by his superior and given the opportunity to rest somewhere close to the front line where he can take his mind off his problems. He will be able to return to the fighting after a few days.[9]

A psychiatric casualty, however, who no longer responds to assistance (encouraging words, embracing, drinking, eating, smoking, alcohol, clear orders, short rests) and upsets other soldiers by his complete collapse, must be given medical treatment at once. Neither his superiors nor his comrades can help him. As already mentioned, his treatment should be carried out in the danger zone so that for him, too, illness cannot be used as an excuse for flight.

Some psychologists want to increase the ability to resist fear by specific preparation for battle. They recommend arousing fears a short time before fighting, for instance by giving a frightening demonstration of the effects of enemy weapons, so that the individual can get accustomed to them, thus developing an antidote, as it were, in the course of an immunization process. They call this 'pre-tension'. We already know that this does not decrease anxiety as a whole, but merely increases it. Hence this method may only be useful in individual cases; in the long run it has nothing to recommend it.

It is possible to lower the level of anxiety by linking the object of fear (as in animal training) with feelings of well-being. This is a treatment used to counter phobias. It is known as 'conditioning'. It is also possible to use hypnosis as a means of keeping people from reacting to objects they fear. Finally, it is possible to take drugs which greatly reduce the physical effects of fear such as rapid heart-beat, vertigo and trembling.

But all these treatments have considerable disadvantages. Everything which diminishes human self-confidence will have undesirable consequences in the long run. All methods of preparation except realistic, informative, anxiety-free training, manipulate, and that, in the end, undermines all self-confidence.

These methods are also rather elaborate. They are hardly suitable for large armed forces. It is also extremely difficult to find the right moment to apply them. Further combat activity is often difficult to predict. Their greatest disadvantage would appear to be the evident ill-will on which their application is based. Every military leader must treat his subordinates as well as possible. They are his only significant assets. Without them, even his machines are useless. Consideration of this kind, which presupposes a deep concern for the individual, is difficult to reconcile rationally or emotionally with the sort of manipulation described above. At the very least it is playing with fire.

In this chapter it has been noted that the number of mentally and physically exhausted soldiers is higher under combat conditions than the number of neuroses. There are many casualties, due to the accumulation of anxieties, and these cannot be removed again completely, even by long periods of rest. Thus increasing pressures lead to more casualties of all kinds. If soldiers under strong pressure are identified in time, if their situation is understood and selective relief applied without allowing any means of 'honourable' flight, this will help to reduce the number of casualties and increase their chances of fighting again soon.

Before examining possible means of manipulating soldiers in order to decrease anxiety or their effects, it is important to summarize once more all the methods available. These should help to give the soldier the will to endure without the need for tricks and gadgets. In the course of this summary, it will be realized that we are far from using all these methods, but that should be our primary aim.

NOTES

1. Report of the War Office, *Committee of Enquiry into Shell Shock*.
2. S.A. Stouffer, *The American Soldier*, Vol. 2, p. 197.
3. Swank and Marchand, *Combat Neurosis: Development of Combat Exhaustion*.
4. S.A. Stouffer, *The American Soldier*, Vol. 2, p. 24.
5. S.A. Stouffer, ibid., Vol. 2, p. 71.
6. S.A. Stouffer, ibid., Vol. 2, p. 453.
7. Swank and Marchand, op. cit.
8. W. Noyce, *They Survived*.
9. S.A. Stouffer, *The American Soldier*, Vol. 2, p. 197.

CHAPTER TWELVE

Summary of Antidotes

All the measures which help the soldier to resist and endure the pressures of combat have been discussed already. It is now necessary to summarize them and to compare their relative importance. A diagram is used to depict this summary. The pressures were depicted by a 'Cloud'. The counter-measures will be shown symbolically by a 'Star of Courage'. It shines brightly and guides the soldier on his way through the chaos of battle. Occasionally the 'Star' is partly or totally obscured by the dark 'Cloud'.

The brightest, and most important part of the star is group integration (chapter 8). If the group is the right size and has sufficient time to grow together under relevant external pressure, cohesion will be achieved and in its wake will grow a group ethic which no member will dare to violate. The group then becomes the focal point in their lives, so much so, in fact, that it hardly matters any more where it is deployed, be it at home or abroad, or for what it is fighting, be it communism or democracy.

But there are drawbacks as well as advantages of strong group integration. The more the group is centred on itself, thus increasing its cohesion, the less it is interested in its environment. An already existing behavioural pattern is thereby reinforced. Neighbouring units, allies, civilians, political systems, and governments become increasingly meaningless. What matters to the group is only what affects it directly. The desire of its members to distinguish the group from other groups is not restricted to insignia and rituals, but leads, in addition, to a spiteful attitude towards others. This attitude occasionally grows into a total rejection of the surroundings.

Almost everybody tries to join a group, be it in peace or war. Therefore, the disadvantages of group cohesion are always present. With strong self-centred groups these increase to some extent. However, in view of the enormous and irreplaceable advantages of group cohesion to the soldier's willingness to fight, the disadvantages must be accepted.

THE 'STAR OF COURAGE'

Group Integration	Hope and Beliefs	Personality
-Primary and Secondary Groups -Group Cohesion (Advantage) -Group Ethics (Conventions) -Group Symbols/Rituals -Pride (Success/Elite) -Inward Looking	-Hope for End of Task -Religion -Illusions (Fanaticism) -Beliefs (Patriotism)	-Self-esteem -Self-reliance -Social behaviour (Optimism/ Dedication/Humour) -Drive -Daring -Intellectual Abilities
Physical Fitness	**Training**	**Leadership**
-Training -Age -Sleep -Food/Drink -Heat/Cold -Smell -Noise -Bodily Activity	-Knowledge ⎫ little is un- -Experience ⎬ known or 　　　　　 ⎭ unexpected -Routine at all levels (Weapons, Staff-Duties)	-Interests of group -Interests of the individuals -Desire for leadership -Coercion

The creation of strong group cohesion must be the primary aim of all methods of organization applied to armed forces. These groups need time to grow into a coherent whole, and they must not be torn apart carelessly. This does not only apply to training and to the first deployment in battle, but also to personnel replacement on the battlefield.

As elite units fight better than other groups, due to their more strongly developed group cohesion, the organization of armed forces should allow sufficient room for them.

Another form of integration can be seen in the relationship between the front-line soldier and the people at home (chapter 8). Girl-friend, wife, parents, children, other relatives and friends are of greater significance than in peace-time. Primarily, this is an emotional relationship, in which love and recognition are of importance for the efficiency of the soldier.

If the people at home do not support a war, it will have an adverse effect on the soldiers' will to fight. The purpose of the war should be acknowledged by everybody and the soldier should be integrated in society.

Almost as important as group cohesion is hope (chapter 6). It has many ways of expressing itself. Very real is the hope for an end to the current operation. It could mean a transfer to the reserve forces, which takes place every 24 hours. It could be time spent in a rest area close to the front, to which one can go after 14 days of operation. It could be the six-monthly leave, or the annual relief of duty from the front. What is important is that the soldier has an attainable, clearly defined and, if possible, unchanging goal before him.

He must not gain the impression of being exploited while others remain at home or are away from the front. Almost everybody is prepared to carry his share of the burden provided others do the same. There should be clear and reliable plans for spreading the load of pressures evenly across the whole group.

Faith also gives comfort and hope to the soldier. In war-time, as in every other crisis in life, interest in religion increases considerably. The chaplain is in great demand.

Frequent flights from reality underline the importance of hope. Many soldiers in desperate situations withdraw into their illusions, which they will sometimes defend fanatically.

It is difficult to judge the importance of the individual personality compared to other factors (chapters 4 and 6). Open-mindedness and a willingness to make contact facilitate integration into the group. Religious faith or strong convictions reinforce resistance to pressures.

It has been noted that drive, independence, self-esteem, intelligence, education and humour also help in resisting the major pressures of battle. This was particularly evident in persons who had to endure great hardships almost or completely alone, such as leaders or survivors from shipwrecks.

In one sense, therefore, the individual personality seems to be of decisive significance, while in another it also appears to be dependent on external factors such as physical deprivations or over-stimulations. During a military operation, it is the leader who is particularly isolated, and therefore it is he who has to rely on his own personality more than any other. His personality must be examined further. At this point, it suffices to say that any selection of personnel must seek to match personality with future tasks.

The individual factors of physical fitness for combat are frequently incorrectly assessed, as their implications are not understood in time of peace (chapters 4, 6, and 7). In this way, physical training and sporting abilities are frequently over-valued. Of course, sport is an excellent means of accelerating group integration and there is no doubt that physical fitness is helpful in many combat situations, for example when an obstacle has to be overcome or heavy loads have to be carried. During an operation, however, those who in peace-time did not excel in any sport may perform just as well as sports champions. When it is a matter of long-term endurance under conditions of deprivation, trained athletes seem to be almost at a disadvantage.

The important factor is that all soldiers need sleep, food and drink, regardless of their physical fitness. If these basic needs are not fulfilled, efficiency and morale will deteriorate rapidly. This is of decisive importance in war. A plate of hot soup will do more sometimes than an encouraging remark or even an impassioned speech.

Noise causes extreme stress. Consideration should be given to wearing earplugs to reduce noise levels.

Activity and exercise are important for the soldier under pressure. Monotony reduces efficiency, as it does in civilian life. Too much rest allows the soldier too much time for worrying (chapter 4). If the soldier is forced to remain absolutely still while under great and continuing pressures, such as sustained fire, he will soon reach a point where he cannot bear it any longer and where he will begin to act irrationally (chapter 7). For such a situation, the soldier has to be taught during training that bodily activity of any kind, as well as shouting and shooting, will enable him to carry on longer.

Finally, it becomes clear again that age and even experience tend to be a disadvantage as far as front-line combat is concerned. Well-trained young soldiers fight more aggressively than seasoned veterans of war.

Peace-time armies should always endeavour to ensure that the non-commissioned officers and the officers at battalion level are as young as possible. (Of course, it is possible that leaders and subordinates might be too young.) It was not possible to determine this lower age limit during this research. This was of no great concern, as the real problem is to be found at the other end of the age scale.

Good training is realistic training. Its main effect is a reduction of the fear of the unexpected and the unknown (chapter 4). Nothing that the soldier may encounter during an operation must surprise him, including his own symptoms of anxiety. In that way, he will become more confident.

Military drill, which facilitates weapon-handling by an acquired routine, or which enables a team to cooperate smoothly in small tactical tasks, will encourage success not only through efficiency, but through the confidence that any kind of routine inspires. One recognizes the familiar and one is at home with routine. The order of routine is a blessing in the disorder of battle.

Everybody recognizes the importance of good training. It is not disputed, although it must be said that it does not achieve the significance of other segments of the 'Star of Courage', which we have already discussed. Considered in connection with the other points of the 'Star', it is evident that training, too, is an excellent means of achieving group integration, strengthening of the personality and improved physical fitness.

Finally, leadership is part of the 'Star of Courage' (chapter 6). It is almost impossible to determine its overall influence. On the one hand, the leader helps in achieving the interests of the group and the individual. He enforces the written and unwritten laws. And he fulfils the need for leadership, which most people feel to some degree in times of crisis.

The leadership influence is very variable, however. Some groups are capable of accomplishing a given task almost without it. In other cases, the leader may have to resort to brute force to make sure his orders are followed. The latter case requires an almost superhuman effort from him. Therefore, in certain instances, the leader may acquire a decisive importance, as some crises may not be overcome without him. He has to be selected and trained with such situations in mind. This is discussed in the next chapter.

All the points of the 'Star of Courage' are arranged around the circle of trust. This is meant to indicate that trust is central to the achievements of the soldier in combat, and that every segment of the star must contribute to building this trust. The group, the people at home, religion, the structure of the personality, the satisfaction of physical needs, training and leadership, all help to build the necessary trust or reinforce self-confidence.

It is difficult to compare the importance of the points of the star. If such an attempt is made, one obtains the graph shown below. The solid lines describe actual significance, while the dotted lines indicate the range of possible increases in significance, depending on the situation.

After due consideration of the 'Cloud of Pressure', the 'Lake of Exhaustion' and the 'Star of Courage', it becomes only too apparent that our title 'Hero or Coward' is much too glib and superficial and quite incapable of expressing the processes taking place inside the individual in times of extreme pressure. It is the intention, in this study, to reconsider the various forces which affect the individual soldier and his role in the ensuing power struggle.

A soldier in combat resembles a mountaineer on a rock face who has to rescue an injured comrade. That is his task. He can solve the problem in a variety of ways. First of all, he can do his duty. Or he can abandon his injured comrade, and neglect his duty by seeking to save himself. Finally, he can give up exhausted, and let himself fall to his death. He cannot just stay where he is. Time is a factor, as it is consuming his strength.

The soldier, too, has a task. For instance, he has to attack or defend a hill. He can do his duty or neglect it. He can run away, either physically or in his mind. But he cannot do nothing. Time, too, is his enemy. He must fight or run.

If the mountaineer is very strong, he can climb up the rope and save himself and his injured comrade. A soldier fighting alone can do the same. But he will be the exception. Normally, that task will be too difficult for a single person. Few are strong enough to go it alone, particularly as the weight of the injured man will drag them both down. The average mountaineer will need all his strength to hold on to the rope and his comrade. He needs help.

This help is given by his comrades, who are above him and who will

COMPARISON OF THE SIGNIFICANCE OF THE INDIVIDUAL COUNTER MEASURES

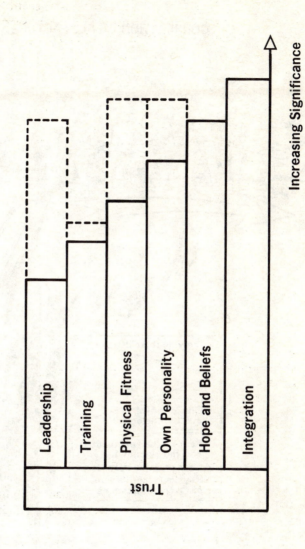

Leadership

Training

Physical Fitness

Own Personality

Hope and Beliefs

Integration

Trust

Increasing Significance

CORRELATION OF ALL FACTORS

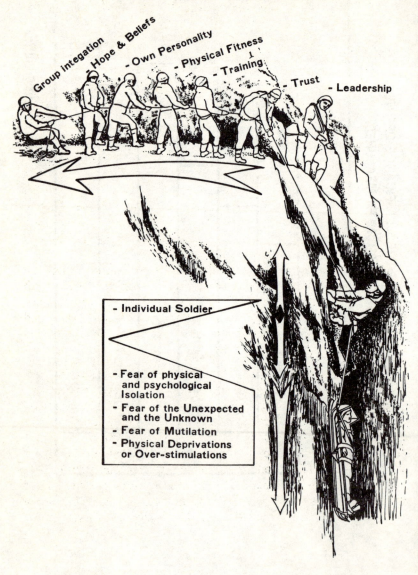

Group integation - Hope & Beliefs - Own Personality - Physical Fitness - Training - Trust - Leadership

- Individual Soldier

- Fear of physical and psychological Isolation
- Fear of the Unexpected and the Unknown
- Fear of Mutilation
- Physical Deprivations or Over-stimulations

pull him up. He can allow himself to be pulled up, or he can assist. For the soldier, these comrades represent group integration, hope and belief, personality, physical fitness, training, trust and leadership.

The weight of the injured person continues to affect the mountaineer. This weight, to the soldier, is called fear of physical and psychological isolation, of the unexpected and the unknown, of mutilation and physical deprivation or over-stimulation.

Both the mountaineer and the soldier are tempted constantly to let go of their heavy burden in order to get themselves to safety more quickly. But what would be said by his comrades, who are pulling him up? Would they still continue to help him? That is his conflict. Therefore, he holds on to the injured man for as long and as best he can and lets himself be pulled up.

Apart from the mountaineer, the injured man, and the comrades pulling up the rope, we have the leader. He considers the scene. He has to evaluate whether the task can be carried out, whether the men need help and whether the man on the rope needs additional assistance. The leader could help in the pulling, for instance, or he could encourage the soldier on the rope.

If the leader misjudges the situation, the injured person may fall to his death, together with the man on the rope, perhaps, or even with the entire group. He himself might perish if he decides, for instance, to help and, in order to inspire confidence, ties himself to the end of the rope. Comparisons with the performance of a group of soldiers under operational conditions are obvious.

The individual certainly has some influence on his own behaviour. A man can decide whether he wants to fight courageously or run away like a coward. On the whole, however, the influence of his instincts, passions, his 'voice of conscience' and the physical conditions are stronger than any decision based on will-power and reason. The most important motivating force is therefore not the Ego but the Id and the Super-Ego. The unconscious and the sub-conscious determine the behaviour of the individual. Whether the individual succeeds or not depends on how many points of the 'Star' remain partly or wholly unobscured by the 'Cloud' and are able to continue shining.

CHAPTER THIRTEEN

Effects on the Commander

In chapter 9 a summary was given of the pressures that both the commander and his subordinates have to bear. In chapter 12 those aspects which enable soldiers to withstand stress were examined. Now we must investigate whether the leader, too, can rely on these same antidotes to extreme pressures.

To begin with, we should consider a few selected, general human reactions which always affect the leader. In addition there are a number of possible individual weaknesses which a leader will have either by inheritance or because of his upbringing and education. They will strongly determine any decision he might make. But in the context of this general discussion they are not considered. They have been studied elsewhere on the basis of historical examples.[1]

One of the reactions is explained by that author in one of his lectures in the following way:

> If one sees a thin, correctly dressed and slightly introverted man, and if one were asked to make a guess, based on appearance, as to whether this man were a librarian or a farmer, everybody would intuitively say a librarian. But that is not a logical decision, since there are many more farmers than librarians. The probability that the thin, correctly dressed, slightly introverted man is indeed a librarian, is low. The logical choice would be farmer.

Man is by nature almost incapable of thinking in terms of statistics. Only after long training will he be able to improve his feel for figures.

Another important reaction concerns the process of decision-making. It was noted in chapter 8 that the desire for love, friendship, sympathy, recognition, respect and power are man's strongest motivations. They influence decisions to such an extent, and mainly unconsciously, that a man will often not do what is logical or necessary, but will allow himself to be led by those desires. One of Dr Dixon's examples illustrates this fact:

> At the end of the sixties, an aircraft exploded in flight en route from Tokyo to Hong Kong near Mount Fujiyama. This holy mountain of Japan is usually shrouded in cloud. Sometimes, however, heavy storms disperse these clouds, and the mountain can be seen in all its majesty. But it becomes particularly dangerous to aircraft, because of the high winds. All this was known to the experienced captain. But he left his course to give his passengers a closer look at Fujiyama. He wanted to do them a favour, he wanted to gain their liking and recognition, and in this process he perished with all his passengers.

Such examples are confirmed by daily experience. Anyone studying on a Monday the reports of the previous weekend's road accidents will find indications that in at least half the cases drivers took risks which in a rational moment they would not have done. They tried to impress others, and thereby they over-taxed themselves and their vehicles in an irrational way.

Connected with this is the desire not to reverse a decision once it is taken. Nobody wants to make mistakes, because that would damage one's reputation. Everybody seeks confirmation of a decision taken (again, mostly subconsciously) and therefore suppresses for as long as possible any new information which contradicts his former decision.

We are all familiar with the smoker who does not want to admit that his habit is risking his health, and who seeks confirmation in newspaper articles, for instance, that his behaviour isn't really that illogical. We also know that after buying a new car we like to dwell on its good aspects and do not care to be reminded of any bad points or that another car may indeed be better. If such a realization cannot be repressed, because dramatic consequences have resulted in the meantime, a radical change of attitude may occur in conjunction with renewed repression.

Finally, it should be noted that most men live by their experiences. It would not be possible for any man to analyse all his future actions before he reaches a decision. He would be overburdened. Therefore, he makes decisions unconsciously, according to what he has always done or experienced. If he is questioned about such a decision, he will reply at once: 'That has always been the case, we have always done it that way'. In most cases, therefore, we decide in accordance with predetermined patterns. These we sometimes mockingly call prejudices, but that underestimates their importance. Prejudices only apply to the extremes.

Because man reacts in this way, it is important that he should have a chance to gain as many experiences as possible which are important for his decisions. It is also essential to 'intellectualize' the decision-making process involving major problems. This is the idea behind any military appreciation.

In addition to these everyday reactions, one also has to contend with the reactions to the pressures of a combat situation. These have been described already. Stress narrows our ability to perceive. It produces an effect similar to wearing blinkers or being in a tunnel. Thus deep-sea divers, who, because of their dangerous profession, can to a certain extent be compared with soldiers in combat, often fail to recognize things which appear on the edge of their field of vision.

Fear also reduces the ability to think. Often the consequences of a decision made under pressure are not apparent to the person concerned. The military saying 'Any decision is better than none at all' will lead to an increasing number of wrong decisions the longer the battle lasts.

Extended periods of pressure lead to over-reaction. That too, will increase the number of wrong decisions. Over-reaction also leads to inconsistency, which can cause a soldier to give an order, cancel it quickly, and then re-issue it again.

Finally, fear and exhaustion reduce the willingness to make decisions at all. There is a tendency to postpone or to avoid them.

These remarks are not intended to belittle the importance of the saying 'Any decision is better than none at all'. It is only intended to point out that the number of wrong decisions rises rapidly under increasing pressures and that anyone suffering from mounting exhaustion and required to make decisions will eventually become totally incapable of making them.

Consequently, decisions of great importance should not be made under physical and psychological pressure. Those having to make decisions should be subjected to as little pressure as possible. If that cannot be achieved, those personnel should be relieved of duty before they reach the stage of extreme excitability or total exhaustion. One important means of slightly reducing the number of wrong decisions made under pressure is 'intellectualizing' the decision-making process.

These considerations have provided the basis for an examination of the personality of the leader.

He has to make the correct decision and he must enforce it. At the same time, he must be able to resist the pressures of combat for as long as possible. The intellectual abilities and characteristics required in the ideal leader in order to minimize the adverse effects of the reactions described above, become apparent. It is not necessary to collect and describe all these essential abilities and characteristics in this book.

By acting like a filter, as it were, this will assist in discovering to what extent the points of the 'Star of Courage' may also shine upon the path of the leader and guide him.

Group integration, so important for the soldier, can do little for the leader. In any case, he cannot be fully integrated into the group which he is leading, and his connection with the group to which he belongs by rank is rather loose, because of his need to be elsewhere much of the time.

Full integration into any group would be a disadvantage in that the behavioural requirements made by group ethics could affect his intellectual ability to make the right decisions. No one can be completely free from the influence of the group's laws, but the leader should be able to analyse them critically so that he can influence them if necessary. In this way, for example, rejection and subsequent isolation of completely exhausted members of the group as simply being cowards must not be allowed.

A close connection with the people at home, as some form of small compensation for weak group integration, becomes important for the leader.

Hope for an end to the operation, personal convictions, and religion can also help the leader. Nonetheless, he must not rely upon them to the same extent as his subordinates do. The crucial difference is represented by the factor of illusion, which is part of all hope, but which must not affect him. Illusion would adversely influence aspects of his intellectual and personal abilities such as open-mindedness, ability to think logically and laterally, self-confidence, daring and initiative.

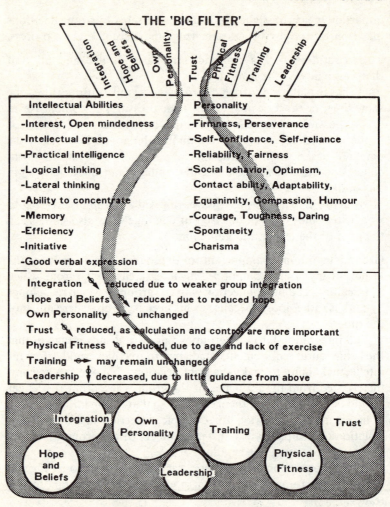

THE 'BIG FILTER'

Integration — Hope and Beliefs — Own Personality — Trust — Physical Fitness — Training — Leadership

Intellectual Abilities
-Interest, Open mindedness
-Intellectual grasp
-Practical intelligence
-Logical thinking
-Lateral thinking
-Ability to concentrate
-Memory
-Efficiency
-Initiative
-Good verbal expression

Personality
-Firmness, Perseverance
-Self-confidence, Self-reliance
-Reliability, Fairness
-Social behavior, Optimism,
 Contact ability, Adaptability,
 Equanimity, Compassion, Humour
-Courage, Toughness, Daring
-Spontaneity
-Charisma

Integration ⬊ reduced due to weaker group integration
Hope and Beliefs ⬊ reduced, due to reduced hope
Own Personality ➡ unchanged
Trust ⬊ reduced, as calculation and control are more important
Physical Fitness ⬊ reduced, due to age and lack of exercise
Training ➡ may remain unchanged
Leadership ⬇ decreased, due to little guidance from above

Integration — Own Personality — Training — Trust — Hope and Beliefs — Leadership — Physical Fitness

Those personal abilities and characteristics which help the individual in the group to bear the pressures of combat also help the leader. His own personality, therefore, is also of decisive significance.

A leader cannot perform the complex task assigned to him without trust in his subordinates. However, it must not be allowed to turn into 'blind trust', even if the subordinates feel this for their leader.

A leader must control his men and act in a calculated manner. Trust must not be allowed to interfere with this.

Moreover, a leader will be able to build up only occasionally the sort of trust with his superiors which exists at the lower levels of the small combat group. In most cases those hardships endured together in close contact, and thus binding, will not exist. A leader will count himself lucky if he succeeds in establishing some form of trust between himself and his superiors. Such trust may give him an extra incentive to carry on.

A leader must also keep physically fit. In this, he is usually at a disadvantage because he is older than his men. Moreover, as a result of his specific duties, he will rarely be able to take physical exercise. Hence stress reactions will affect him more than his subordinates.

As regards training, the leader need not be at a disadvantage.

It is true that his task is more complex than that of the subordinate. There are few situations where the leader can blindly follow the training manual. By way of relevant intensive training it is possible, however, to give him so much knowledge and experience that he learns to trust in his own abilities.

A leader may expect only rarely the same sort of intensive leadership from his superiors that he has to exert towards his subordinates.

This is due to the nature of the hierarchy; the leadership effort tends to become more and more a matter of intellectual decision-making, the higher the level of command, and direct contact with the subordinates is steered away from emotional values towards intellectual abilities. Thus every leader dispenses more emotion to his subordinates than he is able to receive from his own superiors.

If one now considers what remains of the 'Star of Courage' in the way of help for the leader and also brings in the 'Comparison of the Significance of the Individual Antidote', one realizes that most of the things which helped the subordinate to resist the pressures of combat are, or should be, meaningless when applied to the commander.

In the final analysis, the leader can rely completely only on his own personality. He is under greater pressures than all the others, and it becomes apparent that for the choice of a leader personality traits are of decisive importance. Good training may also help him.

In all the other areas he is at a considerable disadvantage to his subordinates. He receives less support from integration, hope and belief, trust and physical fitness, and he must be able to carry on, even when there is little leadership from above. Hence everybody should support him wherever possible. He needs it more than anyone else.

This chapter is concerned with outlining those general human reactions which influence leadership decisions. We do not think well in figures. We depend on love, friendship, sympathy, recognition, respect and power. We obstinately defend decisions which we have made and we live by experience almost exclusively.

Furthermore, stress focuses our powers of perception in an atavistic manner, as if we were wearing blinkers. It reduces our ability to think, induces us to over-react and, ultimately, diminishes our willingness to make decisions. Having to contend with these disadvantages, the leader is not even able to obtain the support which is available to his subordinates. For him, all that he can rely on is his own personality and his abilities. The leader carries the greater burden with less support, and therefore, everybody should concentrate their efforts on helping him in particular.

NOTE

1. N. F. Dixon, *On the Psychology of Military Incompetence.*

CHAPTER FOURTEEN

Consequences for Personnel Selection, Organization, Equipment, Training, Education, Leadership and Tactics

Before beginning to draw a large number of individual conclusions, it is necessary to discover whether any general guidance can be given. This can be done by answering the question: 'How will a future armed conflict be decided?'

There is only one answer: The conflict will be decided by a relatively few men in the front line. This has not changed since the introduction of national mass armies and the machine gun. Further dramatic developments in weapon systems will involve more and more soldiers further to the rear, and more civilians will become embroiled in the fighting. But their participation will be passive. Active fighting can be undertaken only by combat troops. And only a few of these soldiers will decide the outcome of delaying actions, defence and above all of attack at the focal points. Modern technology will make no difference to this as long as weapons have to be operated by soldiers, who by doing so must bravely risk their lives.

If one looks further into the future, then it can be imagined that it will be possible with very sophisticated sensors to detect any enemy target. As a result of this they could be destroyed with weapons which will themselves locate and hit them. But even in the unlikely event that these reconnaissance aids could be used or these weapons launched from a safe distance, the battle is not yet won. The object is to impose one's will on the enemy. The killing of enemy soldiers can only contribute to this. It will still be necessary to leave one's own secure base to occupy enemy territory. Only in this way can he finally be made to surrender. For this, even in such an extremely unlikely futuristic scenario, combat troops will still be needed. In the longer term no change is likely.

The conclusion from this is clear: Victory will be gained only by the side which concentrates on the maintenance or improvement of the will to fight of the front-line soldier, the quality of his physical and psychological abilities, his weapons, his equipment, his training, his supplies, his tactics, and his command. Thus it is not only a matter of incorporating the front-line soldier into his group or giving him comprehensive training. It is a matter of focusing all the psychological and material resources of the armed forces on him.

Every decision made by military management or technologists must have the front-line soldier in mind. Thus selection of personnel at all levels from enlistment to appointments of top commanders must be made to this end. A man who has proved himself in battle should be given priority when decorations are awarded and promotion is being considered. Perhaps in wartime special recognition of this sort should be given only for deeds in battle.

Successful armed forces have always been fighting machines which focused all their efforts on the man who did the decisive fighting for all at the risk of his life. Peace-time forces easily forget this. Thus the infantry certainly does not get enough good recruits. Regimental duty is not rated any higher than staff work. Personal characteristics become increasingly unimportant for selection of personnel and frequent changes of personnel hinder good group cohesion.

Armed forces develop a very strong social structure, without which they could not exist. Therefore any change needs time. It is true that because of the nature of their organization rapid changes in their physical structure can be carried out. However the character of the organization and the mental attitudes of its members can be changed, if at all, only over a long period and with great care. Armed forces are not inanimate objects, like buildings which can be rebuilt if desired. They are living beings, which must be tended like plants with care over long periods until they bear fruit. Thus mistakes made in peace-time are very difficult, if not impossible, to rectify at the time of the greatest crisis in war.

The recognition of this as the highest priority should not however, mean that other important factors are neglected. In order to prevent a possible misunderstanding the significance of the ratio of quality and quantity must be considered.

There is no doubt that a motivated and well-trained soldier fights considerably better than an impressed fighter only given cursory training for his job. But this is not a question at issue for the Warsaw Pact or NATO in Europe.

The investigations so far show clearly that motivation depends very little on a given political system, but primarily on group cohesion. Hence it can be assumed that the soldiers of the two different political systems can be equally well motivated, and this is in fact so. It has also been shown that the significance of long training is overestimated. It is not true that a national serviceman with 18 months' service is much inferior to a volunteer who leaves after three years.

In consequence there will be little more difference between the ability and the will to fight of the fighting forces of the two pact systems than there is between the companies of a battalion or the battalions of a brigade. Elite units will on the whole be above average. This, however, will have little effect on the troops facing each other in Europe, because of the large numbers involved and the fact that they are only a little better than the rest. Quality alone cannot compete against mass armies, which today are professionally trained, led and equipped.

It is now necessary to consider the two findings together. These are firstly that armed forces have to concentrate on the front-line soldier, and secondly that in Europe at least quality cannot overcome quantity. Then it becomes clear that mass armies can be fought only with mass armies, but that within these mass armies quality must be particularly concentrated in the areas where decisive actions may be fought. At these points in a fight or a war, local superiority can be won by small groups.

After these general considerations, let us start with a summary of the consequences for personnel selection. The central problem is how to determine the particular abilities of the individual soldier in mass armies, so that each is used in the best interests of the whole. It is a matter in particular of selecting the right man for the right job.

A number of unanswered questions still remain. They are considered in chapter 16. Some are concerned with methods of selection. The answers to these can be found relatively easily. The remaining questions, however, concern the best possible use of the abilities of the individual within the overall organization. These cannot be answered without further scientific research.

It has been stated that all efforts must be focused on the front-line soldier. But this is a very broad principle. The difficulties lie in the details.

Even if in principle the best soldiers have to be deployed in areas where their presence will be decisive, this does not help in assessing the best composition of fighting groups themselves. For example, do too many active fighters brought together in a small group hamper each other? Is there an ideal ratio between active fighters and passengers? Is the leader's task affected by having too many active fighters in his group?

Even if it is agreed to deploy active fighters in vital areas, then it is difficult to decide whether infantry, parachutists, armoured corps, armoured reconnaissance or commandos have the most important tasks which would give them a case for claiming the best recruits.

And if it is considered that supporting troops will become more and more involved in actual fighting (see chapter 15) then they must be allowed their share of the best men.

The only certainty is that there are not enough good men available for all these tasks. A chain is only as strong as its weakest link and distribution of good personnel must be balanced.

Personnel selection must on the one hand deal with the front-line soldier as its number one priority. It must contribute to the formation of various elite groups who can have a decisive effect on war. On the other hand it must not in this age of mass armies and long range weapons neglect the other troops. The task of personnel selection is harder than ever before. It can only be resolved after much research and re-evaluation of the tasks of the individual soldier. However the following principles, arising from the present study, may be borne in mind.

In the search for quality, character is more important than intelligence and skills. In the future, fighters will remain more important than the managers or technologists. But the baby must not be thrown out with the bath water. This subject will be discussed in the next chapter.

Character is significant, and it is possible to give a general guideline for the main target group for recruiting. The armed forces are looking in particular for the 'supernormal', the mentally stable personality, who may be a little extroverted, and who looks for satisfaction in group activities. Often his previous way of life gives clear clues. Young men who have belonged to sports clubs, or to the Boy Scouts, or who have learnt over a period how to get along without their parents, often do well later in the military environment. With those who have had problems with alcohol or drugs, who are anxious or pessimistic, who have to contend with family difficulties, who cannot manage their money, or who are loners, caution is indicated. They must be carefully investigated. They could fail under the pressures of battle.

It is also important that relatives and friends should support, directly or indirectly, the choice of career of the young man. They need not necessarily be in full agreement with the military career, but they should approve of occupations which serve the public good.

It has not been intended to give the impression that soldiers can be examined and thrown into a job as one would throw letters in a sorting office into individual pigeonholes. This is exactly what must be avoided. The tests should determine general suitability only. After that however the soldier must be allowed to express his own preferences. The willingness with which he consciously or unconsciously asks for a special task is such an important motivating factor that it should not be over-shadowed by the need to fill a particular post.

If the soldier is given a choice, then he will often allow himself to be influenced by friendships, by the nearness of his home town, or by national bounds. Units thus become social structures with internal and external links. The important relationship to the people at home is improved. The value of the soldier to the armed forces is increased. This possibility of choice results in competition between units. They must look to their laurels, otherwise they may not obtain the number of recruits they need. By allowing this every commander is forced to follow the principles of good leadership.

On the one hand, the examination and allocation of good men to key positions is propagated, on the other freedom of choice is encouraged. Perhaps this apparent contradiction is clarified if one considers personnel management after enlistment in the units.

Even in peacetime the soldier must be assessed continuously by his seniors. The many different situations which a soldier faces in his daily work help to assess him correctly. This assessment is decisive for his advancement. It is in the interests of his unit, but also in his own interest.

In war, individual soldiers have to be relieved from duty because of exhaustion or injury. This means that the decision when to relieve is just as important as personnel selection. Only the leader on the spot can decide this.

As a consequence a large amount of delegation of personnel selection is necessary even in peacetime. It has to be realized that this means relying on the judgement of the commander on the spot. Additionally it is made clear to these commanders that personnel selection is their sole responsibility.

Thus selection can be centralized before the soldiers join their units. After this an overall personnel management system can be maintained. However, the sole responsibility must remain with the units. Its selection of personnel and therefore its personnel management must not be influenced by anonymous central bodies or by administrative and legal complications.

The most important task of the organization is fostering strong group cohesion. For this, the following is vital:

The primary group should not be too large. The ten soldiers of the section are if anything slightly too many. The ideal section has between three and five men. For the consideration of the optimum size however, not only rapid integration of its members is important. Just as important is leadership in battle. Here again, it has been shown that the fighting infantry section in the front-line in defence or attack should comprise only a handful of soldiers, since otherwise they cannot all be observed by their leader and are difficult to employ purposefully. It may be different in the support services. In considering the front-line leader in battle, it becomes clear also that it is difficult to maintain overall supervision and control. One must also expect leaders to become casualties. Therefore, there must be sufficient leaders available. The second in command must be able to take control if his commander can no longer continue. Leaderless groups usually become inactive.

If the other military groups to which the soldier belongs become too big, and he is unable to gain an overall picture of them, or if he feels he is anonymous, then they lose their power of integration. This shows the limits of effective centralization.

The primary group should also be supported by the people back home.

It is helpful if the primary groups get together voluntarily. Thus for example, a member of a group may select a new one, and so take over the responsibility for his integration and his behaviour. The primary group should remain together for as long as possible without change of personnel.

It must be welded together through pleasant or even unpleasant group experiences. The frequency and intensity of these will affect the time taken to achieve group coherence.

The group must be recognizable from outside by symbols and rituals, such as unique uniforms, insignia, special drills or name.

This could be counter-productive. Nevertheless, these practices should not be stopped, because they fulfil a basic need. In order to avoid extremes they can be influenced from above by awarding special privileges and decorations for outstanding deeds.

Finally, any social links within a group which lead to strong group cohesion should not be weakened by the introduction of other relationships. For example, it is dangerous to integrate women into these male groups. The group cohesion will be destroyed if unavoidable romantic attachments start within the small fighting group under pressures.

Retention of strong group cohesion is just as important as its creation. This is difficult to achieve since it may affect the necessary flexibility. Two suggested solutions are:

First, to nurture, in addition to the primary group of at most ten soldiers, the larger groupings of the platoon, the company, the battalion, the brigade, the division and of the arms and services. This can be done by bringing together soldiers who have similar tasks or specialist knowledge. Common ethics also help.

Second, there are changes which cannot be avoided. Group members are wounded, fall sick, go on leave, or attend courses. They should retain their contact with the group as far as possible. For example minor injuries and illnesses can be treated in the area. If somebody has to leave his section to attend a course, it may be possible to facilitate his return.

Even if it is intended to leave the small group together for as long as possible, there is a need for flexibility which results in many changes. These seem incompatible. But often a compromise can be found. Thus it is better to leave whole platoons, companies, battalions and brigades without any change of personnel in combat, until they must be relieved because of exhaustion. Then new personnel can be brought in, battle-seasoned soldiers can be retrained together with 'newcomers', to give them a chance to integrate, and then they can be sent back into action again. This is at least better than trying to integrate replacements bit by bit during action.

This attempt to obtain strong group cohesion, and hence to leave the group together for as long as possible unaltered, should however not be taken to extremes. In war this is impossible anyway, but even in peace-time it should not be forgotten that groups which are left together unchanged for too long are liable to become slack. They can be revitalised by personnel changes.

It is difficult to give general rules since the circumstances vary greatly. In principle, however, each man should stay with his group until his behaviour towards the others has fully run its course. This may be twelve months for a national serviceman or three years for a company commander. Thus, despite group cohesion, promotion can be maintained. On the one hand those with ambition must be given the possibility of advancement or there will be bad feeling. On the other hand this can be a help in planning changes to the group.

For armed forces, of equally vital importance is not only the question of timing the relief of units in the front-line by reserves, and finding the best way of integrating reinforcements into fighting units, but also deciding about the overall number of reserves needed.

Stalingrad and Cassino would have worked out quite differently if just a few fresh forces had been thrown into the fight in the first decisive phases of the battle when both sides, after day-long actions, had to continue even when fully exhausted. During the investigations into these lengthy battles, it became quite clear that a single fresh fighting battalion or division in the first critical phase of the initial battle could have decided the whole thing. But, as in so many other battles, at this moment of total exhaustion, neither side had these relatively small forces available. Therefore they were compelled to continue the battle in the same place for many months.

Thus the organization in a decisive battle must still be able to bring in reserves after some days. In this age of mass armies this will be difficult. However, if adequate reserve forces are not available before the beginning of a war, and cannot be raised later, there is no prospect of victory. One must ask oneself whether under these circumstances a war is worth starting. To summarize, victory will go to the side which succeeds in bringing in fresh reserves during the phase of general exhaustion. This will be after three days to four weeks of intensive fighting.

Considerations of personnel replacements and reserves would be incomplete without discussing the degree of specialization required.

Most armed forces try to avoid overspecialization because of the need for interchangeability of personnel. (Consideration of the possible specialization of individual soldiers follows in the section on training.) Thus they demand of all their soldiers a basic and uniform military knowledge which is designed to ensure the survival of the individual. In addition to this every arm or service has to develop its own particular skill.

However, there is a shortage of well qualified personnel. There are not enough men to man all arms and services. Therefore not all will be able to reach the required standards of training. This has been mentioned already. A possible answer is to form special or elite units.

The basic requirements can be maintained for each arm and service to perform its particular skills. However, special elite units might be used for particularly difficult tasks, such as action behind the enemy lines, a night attack, or an airborne landing. This must not necessarily lead to the preference for elite units at the expense of the others, but if used within reason such a policy will lead to healthy competition. The psychological advantages which derive from membership of a special or elite unit and which lead to improved performances can also be utilized. Naturally, in peacetime these elite units must have an opportunity to distinguish themselves by special duties and they should be allowed to show their individuality by insignia and ceremonies.

Thus, here again, no categorical decision can be made. On the one hand as great as possible a degree of interchangeability must be retained, and on the other hand it pays to have elite units in readiness for especially difficult tasks. The solution lies in a compromise.

And finally, the organization should never physically separate the individual soldier from his comrades. There should be as far as possible no tasks which a soldier must carry out on his own.

This however, has its effects on the equipment.

The weapons systems should as far as possible be so designed that they are operated jointly by at least two men, who preferably have visual contact or at least can communicate with each other.

Also, individual soldiers should not be excluded from the group as for example happens with many armoured artillery batteries, where one or more soldiers follow the armoured howitzer in an unarmoured vehicle. If they cannot all remain together under similar conditions, then another form of organization should cater for them.

'Passengers' who on their own would not contribute to the fighting can be made to participate if they become part of a weapons handling team.

The weapons system should leave some room for bodily activity. If the soldier has to remain immobile under the stress of battle, he will very soon become incapable of carrying out his tasks. If the soldier has to use his physical strength to operate the weapons system, he will be helped to keep going.

Fire is only effective if it hits, or results in a near miss. A study indicates that experienced soldiers, who are not yet fully exhausted, only take cover under enemy fire if the impact point is closer than the effective radius of the shell plus 40%.[1] Everything else is a waste of ammunition. Accuracy of fire is the deciding factor. This must be remembered particularly when using artillery or air power. On the other hand the protection of soldiers and their weapons by armour and cover are just as important.

The psychological effects of weapons must not be underestimated. Noise does not seem to be the major factor although it affects in-experienced soldiers in particular and it contributes to exhaustion. Much more frightening for the inexperienced and experienced alike seems to be smoke and dust since they reduce visibility and hamper orientation. It is unnerving not to be able to see where the shooting is coming from.

And finally, the psychological effects which can be caused by the introduction of new weapons (T38 tank, V1 rocket) must not be overlooked. A gradual introduction of such weapons gives the enemy the opportunity of adjusting slowly to the new situation. If however, large numbers of new weapons appear all at once then his morale is undermined more easily.

Some of the historical examples show that soldiers who are only partially trained can fight successfully and can be highly motivated. It is therefore possible to overestimate the importance of training. On the other hand, all studies show that good training appreciably increases the self-confidence of all soldiers and so reduces their anxiety level. Strong characters may manage without this help. For the average man good training still seems to be helpful. Hence it is worthwhile summarizing what is understood by 'good'.

Training gives an ideal grounding for group formation. Hence it should not be left to an anonymous organization, which after weeks or months disperses individual soldiers to different units. It is better to train all soldiers right from the beginning with their parent units.

Training must be enjoyable, otherwise even a volunteer will be discouraged and later on will have only unpleasant memories. It should be interesting, encouraging and successful.

Monotony, boredom, drudgery, lack of responsibility and irrelevance, which can easily form part of peace-time training, are off-putting. The trainee is not integrated. He looks for satisfaction elsewhere, perhaps outside the barracks, but often within it, for example by drinking, by behaving badly, or by bullying his comrades.

The training must develop dormant personality traits. Many young men who enter the forces have for example never had responsibility. By being given tasks of gradually increasing difficulty they gain self-reliance and determination. Many have never before worked in a group. Working together in a team, in which everybody helps each other, provides a new experience for them and encourages them to show consideration for their comrades.

Military training is often lacking in this respect. Many instructors, because of their own uncertainty or desire for recognition, interfere so much that those under them become slack in their work and no longer pull together.

All training must be realistic, and here the forces, in their constant desire to oversee and control everything, make their most serious errors. Instruction, parade ground drill, and shooting range practice give young soldiers the impression that in the forces everything is well organized. It is only in the large-scale manoeuvres that they realize for the first time that quite often confusion and chaos predominate.

Firstly a young soldier may be surprised that he can see nobody on the battlefield. He cannot make out the enemy, although he may have been informed that they will attack him.

He is deployed somewhere with his group and does not know where his neighbours and his superiors are.

Nothing happens for hours. Then there is a hasty exchange of fire and sudden moves to new positions.

His battlefield experience — the feeling of being cut off, and the inactivity, alternating with hectic action, is often interpreted as an organizational failure in the planning of the exercise. He does not realize that for the first time in his military career a touch of reality has been added.

Many aspects of the battlefield can be reconstructed realistically away from the field of battle, although this may not always be easy. Experience of the effects of fire can be shown in a convincing way not only by setting up targets but also by firing at soldiers in bunkers or over their heads. Excessive safety precautions should not prevent the soldier from gaining such practice. His life may depend on it later.

Training can help considerably in reducing the fear of the unknown and unexpected. Thus, for example tanks should no longer appear as frightening monsters to the infantryman. He must get used to tanks by becoming familiar with them; having one roll over him while he is in a slit-trench, or taking part in anti-tank warfare in built-up areas, are only a part of this. The infantryman should also have the opportunity to travel in a tank with hatches closed down. He should then be given the difficult task of detecting well-camouflaged infantry and then engaging them.

Another possible way of reducing the fear of the unknown and unexpected is to use, in exercises, snipers and enemy units which have infiltrated or even broken through the defensive system. The first time an enemy machine gun opens fire from behind anxiety is increased considerably, even in an exercise. The more this is repeated the more the soldier learns to trust in his group, in the efficacy of his cover, and in his own weapon.

Darkness and fog raise anxieties in everybody, so exercises must also accustom the young soldier to night and to poor visibility.

By using simulated firing and hit equipment such as Talassi or Simfire the soldier learns to turn the terrain to his own advantage. He realizes that the enemy faces problems also, and that he himself has a good chance of survival. These simulations strengthen confidence in his own abilities better than a more or less arbitrary decision by an umpire in an exercise.

Other pressures of battle such as the use of nuclear and chemical weapons, the recovery of the wounded and their treatment, or the fear of mutilation, are difficult, if not impossible to simulate.

However, every soldier and every leader must understand how the resulting fears will affect him, and what will help him to control them. Therefore, procedures which help to reduce fear under pressure should be practised also. Talking to each other, calling out to each other, shouting battle-cries, all sorts of bodily activities, bodily contact, shooting at random, or humour are aids of this sort.

There have been proposals to condition soldiers, by giving them a sort of pre-stressing by exposing them to warlike conditions. This was attempted for a time by the British Army in World War II by overhead shooting, violent films, and visits to abattoirs. The result is doubtful. First, it is preferable to introduce trainees step by step to the pressures of battle. Otherwise fears will develop to such an extent that it may be impossible to remove them. This has the opposite effect to that intended. Second, the terrors of war are so varied and numerous that they cannot all be simulated in peacetime anyway. Simple methods seem to give better results.

Discipline helps too. The daily ritual of shaving may seem to bear little relationship to the accuracy with which a soldier fires a weapons system. However, someone who carries out this simple routine unfailingly tends to find that self-assurance and equilibrium come easier, and this makes it possible for him to use his weapons systems more effectively.

Training must not only be interesting and realistic. It can only give lasting self-confidence if it is also comprehensive. All forces like to have the 'all-round soldier', since he is interchangeable. But they all lack training time and so they concentrate on specialization.

However, a soldier loses his self-confidence if he no longer understands what is happening in his area of vital interests. Thus it is not sufficient if an infantryman knows only how to operate his rifle, his pistol, and his machine gun. He must understand also how anti-tank weapons, hand grenades, mines, flares, radio sets, and the like are operated. Over-specialization can in the end destroy the self-confidence of the individual, and must be avoided as much as possible. Under the pressures of battle, he feels unable to resist the threats he faces, and will soon give up. But he is supposed to fight ... Bearing these points in mind, in the interest of the individual it might be better to set a clear minimum period for National Service. Gradual acclimatization to battlefield conditions becomes possible only in large-scale exercises. These are important not only to front-line troops but also to the soldiers further to the rear. Service troops and headquarters staff must be included because they often lack experience and therefore when surprised in battle situations tend to give in more quickly.

Realistic and comprehensive training does not only motivate, bring out personal qualities, or reinforce self-confidence, it also increases stamina and results in war losing some of its terrors.

Training cannot be enjoyable if the soldier does nothing but take part in lifelike exercises; he also needs rest and recreation. For this reason other group activities such as team games, hiking, mountain climbing, sailing or camp fire entertainment should be used deliberately as an aid to fostering team spirit and developing latent abilities. It is important that the composition of the group and its leader does not change, and that the activities are challenging.

Taking a small group for a walking expedition which lasts several days may be of more value as regards fighting efficiency than a similar period spent on a firing range. The leader must find the right mixture of more formal military training and recreational activities aimed at strengthening the group.

In the light of this, it becomes clear that a top performance by an individual, in sport for example, is not particularly important. One may be proud of him, or he may act as a good example, but fostering the team spirit is more important than supporting the individual. This has consequences when deciding which kinds of sport should be played and encouraged. Competitive team games in which everybody can participate bring better results for the training of armed forces than the challenge produced by individual events.

This leads on necessarily to a consideration of the intensity of military training required. Many commanders advocate a very intensive and demanding schedule which may easily turn into drudgery. So what are the limits?

There are a number of things which cannot be learned. A person's tolerance of fear, of lack of sleep, of hunger and of thirst cannot be increased. In fact to experience fear can even be a disadvantage in the future. It is therefore necessary to give soldiers the opportunity to learn that men can put up with a great deal. During training, a soldier should be made to realize, at least once, that he is capable of withstanding more than he thought. However, if soldiers are stressed to the limits of their endurance, the possibility of teaching them new skills is reduced. An overtired and hungry soldier is no longer interested in how his machine gun should be dismantled and reassembled, or how his vehicle should be serviced and maintained. Heavy physical and psychological pressures reduce the possibilities of successful instruction.

It is better therefore to hold a series of short exercises (36 hours) in which all the soldiers can be trained intensively. More infrequently (perhaps annually) a longer and very strenuous exercise could be conducted in which the men might gain experience of their limits of endurance.

In these exercises, the leader and his group should be put under equal pressure. This compels the commanders to delegate and to organize shifts. Furthermore the leaders and their subordinates are brought together through the pressures which they face jointly.

Those in charge of training must reach a balance between exercises primarily designed to train and those intended to put soldiers under pressure.

It has been pointed out already that sporting activities are often overrated by the military. Every soldier must naturally maintain or even increase his physical capabilities but there is no reason to assume that very good sportsmen make very good fighters. It is true that good team sportsmen are often natural fighters, but the ability to tolerate physical and psychological pressures cannot be correlated to sporting abilities. The value of sport is that, besides increasing these overall physical abilities, it enhances group integration and self-confidence. The psychological effects are more important than the physical. Nobody is advocating a reduction of time devoted to sport. Quite the contrary. But the priorities have been clearly defined. The emphasis is on team games in which everybody can take part.

Finally, the best way to learn is by doing; theory only provides a basis. Training is therefore the continual alternation of theory and practice, an old adage which is often overlooked in this age of universal education.

If for economic reasons, priorities for training are to be set, then the training of the leaders is most important. They bear the heaviest pressures in battle. They alone are responsible for passing on knowledge. They make the most important decisions and the effects of their mistakes are greater than of those made by lower ranks. Taking the group of leaders as a whole, those commanding fighting troops must take first place.

Training and education are inseparable. Since the performance of a soldier is influenced more by his character than his skills, general education is even more important than training. But the one can scarcely proceed without the other. Training is an ideal means of education. Experts may disagree about whether what is done in the forces can really be regarded as education.

A young man's major characteristics are determined early on in life by genetics, upbringing and education. In the military it is mainly a matter of developing those characteristics already present. Education therefore should not repress but encourage them.

Some of the characteristics desirable for soldiers of the future have been discussed already. In particular self-reliance, optimism and self-confidence will be required. These can only be developed if initiative is encouraged and the soldier learns to carry out the tasks allotted to him.

Another aim of education is to instil into the soldier military ethics. There are values which are very important for the forces, such as devotion to duty (acceptance of responsibility, daring, stamina, cameraderie), integrity (incorruptibility, reliability, loyalty) and a sense of responsibility (for country and subordinates). Some modes of behaviour are particularly disliked, such as theft from one's own comrades or avoidance of duties by illness or by surrender to the enemy.

Finally, for the soldier, persistence and the will to carry on are more important than in civilian life. The soldier must try to attain his objective under all conditions: he must not give up. Toughness is demanded of him, both towards himself and others. In battle, a certain amount of coercion both subtle and obvious will be necessary.

Some say that such a code of honour results in the soldier becoming isolated from society in general. This overlooks the fact that tightly-knit groups always have their own moral attitudes. It might therefore be an advantage for society if these attitudes held by the forces are channelled particularly in one direction. It should be possible for the armed forces to make the ethical view clear both inside and outside the forces by honouring soldiers for gallantry in war-time or for good service in peace.

Every leader has to deal continuously with four problems:

He is faced with different sorts of tasks.

Different kinds of ability are required for the solution of these tasks.

The interests of the group change.

The interests of the individual change.

Additional factors which can be influenced by education are shown in the diagram reproduced below.

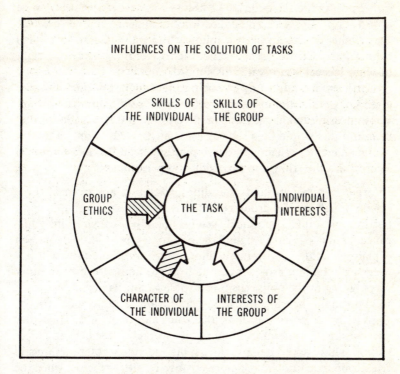

The skills and the interests of individuals and groups do not differ from those in the previous diagram. It is clear that group ethics and the character of the individual have a considerable effect on the ability to solve a task. Their influence can be determined to some extent by education in the same way as skills can be determined by training. This must take place before deployment in battle in order to make the overall task of the leader easier — this is a decisive aid in the pressures of battle.

It is not intended to give the impression that education in the armed forces can much alter a man. Rather the opposite applies. He is so strongly affected by his predispositions and by his subconscious that often there is little point in trying to alter them. It is better to turn them to advantage. Nevertheless, it is particularly important for leaders to make decisions which are as far as possible uninfluenced by these elements. Only in this way is an objective approach possible. It is also helpful to act objectively when making tactical decisions such as 'reviewing the situation'. The ability to think objectively can be improved by guidance and education; intelligence can be fostered. This applies just as much to the military leader as it does to his civilian counterpart. The difference is that the former must never lose sight of what basically motivates his subordinates.

Furthermore, education can help to reduce part of the unwanted effects of the emotional concentration of the soldier upon his group. It is impossible to change this completely, and if one considers group cohesion this would be a serious error anyhow. It is only a matter of changing things slightly by developing an intellectual and emotional interest in other things in the soldier's environment.

In order to avoid misunderstandings, examples are given of these points. Furthermore, group cohesion is so outstanding that in comparison questions of political systems and allies pale into insignificance. Soldiers might even hold them in contempt. Although one can explain to soldiers why these things are important, they will not necessarily be interested. It can be brought home to them in other ways: going to the polls, electing a spokesman, having access to an 'ombudsman', hearing and seeing politicians, and personal friendships with soldiers of the allies, all create emotional links. Thus joint exercises by German and Italian units scarcely alter the prejudices Germans have about Italian soldiers, but individual comradeship and friendship may bring much more positive results — that is, when the exercise is a success. However, these exercises require so much planning and are so costly that they should be considered only where major military requirements or the public interest make them necessary.

One should realize that this behaviour has its advantages even when judged on ethical grounds. A self-contained group, shut off from its allies, cannot readily be incited towards feelings of hatred. Such an attempt would only be worthwhile where a feeling of dislike already existed. It is then possible to direct and to increase this animosity, although within a balanced single personality this would fail.

Education cannot really change a soldier. Therefore, it should bring out and develop the required characteristics and should suppress the negative aspects. A training based on the assumption that only minor changes can be brought about will be more successful than a training which attempts extensive ones. If carried to extremes, breakdowns may be caused. The most common effect is that soldiers withdraw their cooperation either covertly or openly, or leave the armed forces as soon as they can.

These fundamentals of education apply even more to the education of leaders. The first priority is for a military leader to set an example. The leader must not ask his men to perform any tasks which he is not prepared to carry out himself. If this is not the case his subordinates will try to get away with doing and risking as little as possible. He must be capable of fulfilling all demands made on him.

He should also correspond to the ideal of the informal leader: he should be acceptable to the group.

It is not too difficult to satisfy this requirement. It should be remembered that any leader is really elected. The group itself has no right to choose, that is for their superiors. But they make their choice using the same criteria that any other sensible group would apply. It is a matter of an indirect choice.

The leader is to a certain degree dependent on his group. Hence it is important on the one hand that he understands the group and its members, and on the other hand that he can effectively exert his influence. This can be achieved above all by providing information, by putting his points across by convincing speech or by example, by delegating tasks and by concern for welfare. He should make only reasonable demands on his group — unreasonable or incomprehensible orders lead to reluctance. The sharing of responsibility generates interest. Further, the group must know that it can rely on the leader in any circumstances.

The leader is also a father figure, who can impose his own ideas. These thoughts should, however, be compatible with the existing rules and moral attitudes of the group as far as possible. Thus leadership demands much sensitivity and a sound understanding of men.

Leadership is in the first place conviction; subordinates must be convinced intellectually and if possible emotionally. The leader, therefore, must explain what is to be done and give comprehensible information on other matters.

Leadership is also trust. The leader will only be able to convince his subordinates if they trust him. He must gain their trust, for example, by looking after their interests. He must care just as much about their food, sleep and off-duty time as about the recovery of the wounded, properly timed fire support or families back home.

Finally, leadership means coercion. In the interests of all, the leader must ensure that all written and unwritten laws are observed. Mostly, he will be able to do this by convincing his men and by setting an example. But he may be compelled to exert brute force — many a leader will hide a good heart under a hard exterior.

The leader cannot integrate himself with the group which he leads; he is necessarily lonely. Therefore he must have a stronger character than his subordinates. But in order to reach the decisions which only he can make, he needs also the ability to think logically and intensively. It is a help to him if there is a group of other leaders which he can consult from time to time, or if he has staff to advise him.

There should be no way in which a leader can evade his responsibilities. Here the ethics of the group to which he belongs are of help. Still more important is to make him solely responsible for final success or failure. This gives him no chance to avoid his share of the responsibility, or to find scapegoats in case of failure.

Finally, the historical examples have made it clear that in battle very little goes according to plan. Situations change rapidly and unexpectedly. It is nearly impossible to gain a clear and comprehensive picture. Often only the commander on the spot can make out what is going on in his area. Often he is offered unexpected opportunities which if accepted quickly can lead to victory. Future improvements in reconnaissance and communications will make no difference. Therefore, it remains important to delegate tasks and corresponding responsibilities to leaders at all levels.

All the factors so far described have an effect on tactics. In the future an enemy will be forced to give in only if he is physically and psychologically pressed to the utmost. For this, forces must be deployed in a tactically intelligent manner.

The greatest fear of the combatant is the fear of physical and psychological isolation. This fear can be used tactically in two ways: by increasing this fear in the enemy and at the same time giving him a chance to surrender 'honourably', so providing him with a 'let out'. It is very difficult to infiltrate group cohesion. In fact it is easier to destroy the link between group and leader or to infiltrate the relationship between the individual and the people back home. This, therefore, is a priority target for propaganda and psychological warfare.

The weakening or the breaking of the relationship of the individual to the group must be combined with an attempt to make the enemy surrender. He should have no fear of being captured, and he must be made aware that he will be well treated. More than mere propaganda is needed here. It must also be true.

Surrender must be morally acceptable for the individual as well as for the group. It is widely accepted, for example, that it is all right to give up because of lack of ammunition or sudden loss of leadership, thus making it worthwhile to cut off supplies or to kill the leaders.

It is also advantageous to increase the fear of the unexpected and the unknown. Uncertainty will grow if, as in the 'Blitzkrieg', there are unexpected and serious breakthroughs. Supplies and reinforcements can be interrupted, retreat made impossible, and the leadership smashed together with its command communications. Nearly as effective on a smaller scale is the infiltration of a machine gunner or a sniper behind the enemy lines.

This uncertainty can also be created in a seemingly successful attacker who is allowed to make rapid advances and breakthroughs with the result that his forces are split up. This is important, when one considers the Russian doctrine of pressing on with an attack unceasingly until victory is achieved. These attacking forces are then cut off from further supplies and reinforcements by the defenders who remained behind. At the same time, they are attacked from the rear and the flanks, whilst they are contained at the front, so increasing considerably the psychological pressures on the isolated attackers.

Thus by means of camouflage, use of cover, firing drill, in-depth deployment, use of units deployed further to the rear (reserves, artillery, engineers, supply services) and the resolve not to give up positions that have been by-passed or broken through, the attacker is forced into a situation where he can be induced to surrender relatively easily, either individually or in groups. After he has proved his courage in attack, he can be induced to give in for various reasons good or bad such as supply difficulties or failure of weapons and vehicles.

The situation for the defenders is psychologically more favourable, they are knowledgeable about the terrain and the neighbouring forces, they do not have to leave cover so often, the less strenuous activities required for defence are those required anyway of the general mass of soldiers, and plans need not depart too much from reality. The attacker is much more uncertain in such a situation than is the defender and it is tempting to make use of this. It is much more difficult to convince a dug-in defender that it is not worthwhile continuing to fight.

It is also possible to increase the enemy's uneasiness by the use of new weapons; by the arrival at the front of fresh units under conditions of strict secrecy; or by adopting new tactics. However these factors will rarely create as favourable a psychological situation as can the cutting off of an attacker.

The fear of mutilation can also be deliberately increased. This begins with the use of weapons systems which raise fears out of all proportion to their effect. Thus the bayonet has scarcely any value in fighting, but it terrifies. Attacks from the air often lack accuracy; nevertheless, napalm raids in particular are feared. Snipers, who are able to kill only a few individuals, have a psychological rather than a physical effect. In the long term fire which hits or is a near miss has the most frightening effect.

Finally, reserves must be thrown in when both sides are completely exhausted. As indicated earlier, properly timed relief is of decisive importance.

As well as increasing pressures on the enemy, consideration must be given to reducing those same pressures on one's own troops. Delaying actions, attack, and defence put different degrees of pressure on the soldier. Defence is easiest to tolerate. For this reason, tasks of varying difficulty should be given as far as possible to units with the right qualities and which have attained an appropriate standard of training. Whilst it is perhaps possible to defend a sector at low risk by a company with a high and not yet fully integrated reservist component, raids on enemy headquarters should be entrusted only to elite troops.

Pressures on our own forces are diminished by dissemination of the sort of information considered vital for the survival of the group. Plans should be simple and easy to understand and should not be changed too often. All soldiers should be kept up to date about the current situation.

It must be remembered that in all cases and at all times, both sides are only really ready to give up if they can do so without loss of honour. This sense of honour is decisive.

Most of these conclusions are not new. Experience and observations of many years are handed down from one generation of soldiers to the next almost unthinkingly. Thus the British at Calais, the Russians at Stalingrad, and the Germans at Cassino fought heroically without ever having studied the subject in the way that this book attempts to do. The soldiers and their commanders mostly did the right thing in war without knowledge of psychology, sociology or statistics. In particular, those forces with strong traditions committed relatively few major errors.

This study has also shown that those who were able to make in-depth studies of their fellow men or of themselves in order to understand their behaviour, and to draw conclusions from it, were on the whole more successful in command than those who depended only on conventional military wisdom.

Man has not changed. Since the time of the French Revolution with its 'levée en masse' (national army) and the introduction of the machine gun with the need for dispersal, the battle situation for the front-line soldier has basically remained the same. Technology has merely accelerated everything – the leadership process, exhaustion and death. Therefore, there is little in this book that can be new.

It can present only what many military leaders know and practise already, and thereby arouse and encourage the understanding of human behaviour on which success in war depends.

Also it can ask whether important changes may be expected in the future (chapter 15).

Finally, it adopts a systematic approach which makes it possible to compare and weigh up the most significant factors.

This chapter is rather long, because of the many necessary 'ifs and buts'. The number of relevant findings for the fighting forces in Europe is however not very large:

– All efforts should be concentrated on the front-line soldier.
– Mass armies can be fought successfully only by other mass armies.
– Elite units should be used only for special tasks which cannot be carried out easily by standard formations.
– Reserves will have more significance in future.
– Only purposeful recruitment and continued personnel selection during training will ensure that the right man is in the right job.
– Character is more important than intelligence and abilities.
– The individual should have a say in his postings.
– Personnel management is best delegated to the level of company and battalion commanders.

- The main aim of the organization should be the creation and the maintenance of group cohesion (size of groups, fluctuations, jointly experienced challenges, possibilities for promotion).
- Fighting forces need a certain degree of support from the people back home.
- Technology must be designed around the person (things to take into account are: isolation, an active role for 'passengers', freedom of movement, noise, restricted vision).
- Fire is only a paying proposition if it hits or at least nearly does so.
- Training should be practical, motivating, realistic, relevant and comprehensive.
- Individual over-specialization can undermine self-confidence.
- Education and training should be concerned especially with bringing out dormant abilities.
- Education helps to teach the soldier group ethics.
- Leadership is information, motivation, trust and coercion.
- The leader is more heavily pressured than his subordinates. Therefore, he needs much more strength of character than they do.
- The leader should bear the full and undivided responsibility at all times.
- Leaders at all levels should have appropriate tasks and responsibilities delegated to them. Only in this way can any opportunity be grasped.
- The defender can make particularly good tactical use of the attacker's fears of isolation, the unexpected and the unknown.
- The enemy should always be given the opportunity to surrender without feeling dishonoured.
- Every soldier must know the pressures which he faces in action, and how to control his fears.

It can be assumed that all fighting forces in Europe take these factors by and large into account, and therefore that they have attained a relatively high level of efficiency.

There may be some slight differences, which cannot be altered. Thus the degree of self-sufficiency of the soldier and the leader at all levels depends on education and political systems. The possibility of using coercion depends on social conventions.

There will also be differences because of carelessness, negligence, superficiality or careerism. The side which is numerically greatly superior may neglect some of the fundamentals and yet survive or even win a war. However, for those who are numerically inferior at the outset like the NATO forces, such a failure will lead to defeat.

In preparing the fighting forces for the pressures of war, the temptation is to go to extremes. But in most of these preventive measures what matters is to maintain a constant and balanced course.

Group cohesion is the decisive factor for combat efficiency. But concentrating on it alone would soon make the fighting force unbalanced. Thus elite units will always have a part to play, but they should not be promoted at the expense of others. Thus although highly technological fighting forces need some specialization, this can put additional pressures on the individual in battle. It is difficult not to be influenced by fashionable trends, or to resist the temptation for self-advertisement by introducing revolutionary ideas or measures. But none of the conclusions suggested by this study are very spectacular. Their implementation should be balanced and restrained, and requires continuous effort at the lowest level.

Finally this chapter has shown that the effectiveness of the fighting forces depends almost entirely upon their military leaders. If leaders at all levels select their subordinates properly, motivate them, train them and equip them well, and lead them successfully, then no power from outside the armed forces can gain any important influence. Although some may not wish to admit it, the pivot of military morale is and remains the primary group. Its rules cannot be changed at random. Therefore we must build on it.

We should stop making others responsible for past, present, and future failures of the armed forces. We soldiers carry the undivided responsibility.

NOTE

1. P. Watson, *War on the Mind.*

CHAPTER FIFTEEN

Future Prospects

Forecasting the future is not easy and many pundits disagree with each other. Here, we will confine ourselves to assessing the level of future pressures on the soldier. This is easier than the general question of how the future will look.

In studying this, we must not only concern ourselves with the front-line soldier, who up until now has been under the heaviest pressure. If we think of the Russians who in Stalingrad crossed the Volga under enemy fire, or of the parachutists who in Cassino had to withstand overhead bombardments for hours and hours, then we must ask ourselves if it is possible to bear even greater suffering. From now on, the support troops of all kinds will have to be considered as well. In a future war they will perhaps also be more highly involved than hitherto, and their importance as to the outcome of a future battle may be increased.

With regard to the possible scenarios of future wars, a range of possibilities is in store for the soldiers of European countries. Basically the following possibilities exist. They may arise individually, simultaneously or consecutively.

Because of its horrifying effects for everyone, 'total war' between the Warsaw Pact and NATO must be considered first. The result would be mass armies, weapons with effects which have never been experienced before, or are so far unknown: especially chemical, nuclear, and perhaps biological weapons. The civilian population would be heavily involved. All countries would make full use of the mobility of their troops. Hence there would be no static or even stable front. Some countries would be quickly overrun with serious future consequences. In general a relatively short war of days or at most a few weeks is expected. Much of this picture may be wrong. The use of nuclear, biological, or chemical weapons is not inevitable. Mobile warfare may remain the dream of those responsible for teaching tactics. The duration of the war cannot really be forecast, even if one considers the known levels of existing supplies. (If the NATO deterrent remains effective, this war will probably never happen.)

The recognizable consequences of a future war which lie within our consideration are the use of mass armies, the large increase in numbers of weapons and their effects, the involvement of practically all the soldiers and many civilians in the fighting, and the possible break-up of connected military fronts.

A second conceivable scenario is an attack by the Warsaw Pact on a single NATO country, with the objective of occupying it. This could be done by making use of a period of weakness in the Alliance, and by simultaneously giving security guarantees to any country not directly involved whether it be inside or outside NATO. Strategists describe this as 'limited war'. As far as the invaded country is concerned the situation would be different from that of the first scenario only in so far as it would have to expect a swifter and more thorough enemy penetration and a shorter war. If the attacker is greatly superior in conventional weapons and if the defending country has no nuclear capability of its own, the probability of the use of nuclear and chemical weapons might be reduced. In studying the pressures involved in this scenario, it is significant that the defending soldiers would very soon face defeat. This may soon convince them that further fighting is not worthwhile. Therefore, the attackers would probably succeed very soon in bringing the defenders to heel.

Both scenarios can be extended by actions of a fifth column or guerillas. However, in the view of some forecasters guerilla action may also develop independently, because in this way they may undermine the potential of the super-power, and also smaller, but active groups in a country hold out the possibility that they may be capable of taking power. This type of warfare is not very promising in densely populated countries such as those in Europe which are relatively easily surveyed and controlled. Therefore, it is in the author's opinion unlikely. Fifth column activities accompanying a limited war are more probable. Such a force was deployed in the rear of the defending soldiers at Calais, and increased their fear of the unknown and the unexpected. The impact was greatest on those who were not strongly contained within their groups, or on those who were fighting in a position where they were unable to view the situation as a whole.

Additionally, some of the soldiers of NATO countries must expect to serve outside NATO territory, e.g. in the Middle East as a peace-keeping force, or as reinforcements for troops already operating there. In such cases a strange environment and unusual climate bring considerable further pressures.

Finally, many NATO forces may be used for internal policing duties. This puts a considerable strain on each individual.

Such service can affect the individual's self-esteem; he must take action against his own people. If large numbers of the population were to organize protests in support of aims with which the soldier sympathizes, a partial or total break-up of the armed forces could result. Iran and Afghanistan are recent examples of this. In comparison, actions against small extremist groups result in less pressure.

Also the nature of the task is strange to the soldier. He has learnt that in war the enemy has to be fought with the most powerful weapons available. Now, however, he has to use as little force as possible. Because of this difference, it is not recommended that soldiers should jump from the first situation to the second. They should be able to adapt gradually but this may lead to further pressures. Here again, it may be considered better to use separate and properly trained units held in readiness for these different tasks. The task of the Armed Forces of the Federal Republic of Germany is easier, since the constitution does not permit them to undertake any real police role.

Thus, the range of possibilities which may confront the soldiers of European states in the future is wider than ever before. Their professional task becomes increasingly complex.

These multiple roles also have to be carried out under changing political and sociological conditions.

Many of the duties can only be understood if political relationships are considered. Thus NATO strategy is mainly political − it is intended for deterrence rather than war. Therefore, it can be built on an apparent contradiction. It threatens the potential attacker with defeat by the use of nuclear weapons − which would cause the destruction of both countries. A politician used to political manoeuvring may find such thinking plausible, but a soldier who has strong emotional links with his group and a more straightforward view of honour is easily confused.

In addition, the politicians themselves are increasingly influencing the professional decisions of the soldiers. The continual interventions of the US President during the Vietnam War are an example. This is one extreme; at the other end of the spectrum are the debates in the West German parliament on the length and content of a training course for corporals.

Finally, the public is becoming more aware of professional military matters. Levels of education, interest in community affairs and often a desire for publicity, are all on the increase, with the result that many civilians express concern about the armed forces, even when its task is limited to defence against external aggression and it consists only of a voluntary recruited force. The frequent publicity given by the media is partly responsible for this. This book is not concerned with these developments. It is only intended to indicate that the soldier in future will be confronted with a wider range of tasks than ever before. In fulfilling these duties he will be affected to a great degree by political or sociological considerations.

Next we may ask who in the future, under these conditions, will want to take up a military career? Who will sign up for a number of years or for life? A person's origins and motives are of particular interest.

It is difficult to find any answer, and certainly generalizations cannot be made. There will probably still be differences between countries, reflecting their different histories. The answer may depend on the number of recruits needed. The smaller British Army, for example, may continue to recruit its officers from the relatively well-off upper middle class whilst the West German Army, which is numerically much greater, may continue to be a means of social advancement. There will also be differences between the individual branches of the armed forces. The more technically orientated air forces will certainly attract different men from those attached to the army.

Although no comprehensive studies are available, there seems to be a general tendency for the majority of recruits to come from the rather more conservative rural areas or small towns. This may perhaps be explained as follows. These areas support the government, if not the party in power, almost without reservation. They consider themselves supporters of the State, and have no interest in revolutionary changes. They regard the observance of law and public order as important, and include many social climbers. Their sons fit relatively easily into the military hierarchy, and find that its discipline and predictability provide a reassuring or even pleasant environment.

If the social prestige of the military profession in Europe does not alter appreciably, this type of recruit will continue to predominate, and will greatly influence the thinking and the behaviour of the armed forces.

Many psychological and sociological studies have compared military groups with similar civilian groups. Not only do these studies confirm that military groups are relatively conservative; soldiers have been shown to manifest a remarkably high degree of normality. Some researchers have found this striking enough to be characterized as 'super-normal'.

It is interesting that this finding also applies to groups of soldiers who have been accepted by the forces without any sort of psychological test, and later promoted. Thus nervous, unstable and unsociable men are consciously or unconsciously rejected by those making personnel selection, even when they apply no scientific methods, and this result is likely to be self-perpetuating.

A change in the background and behaviour of the professional soldier in all levels of the services is unlikely, despite the dreams of some idealistic sociologists and politicians. These soldiers of the future will integrate well into their primary and secondary groups. Because of their background, they should have little difficulty in operating the increasingly complicated weapons systems. It probably remains important especially for the officers, that they should feel they are making a worthwhile contribution to their country and their people. This desire can be the decisive factor when choosing a military career. They may not feel like talking about it, concepts such as the 'motherland' and 'patriotism' might even be embarrassing to them. Nevertheless they will wish to work for society. In battle this feeling either vanishes rapidly, or at least becomes less apparent among other emotions.

A certain reluctance to change will remain. Extreme reactions are scarcely to be expected. The current code of honour is not likely to alter appreciably. These trends help the armed forces as a whole in the execution of the difficult tasks allocated to them.

Officers, non-commissioned officers and soldiers with such a motivation must feel some revulsion towards the new tasks described above and towards political and social developments. They do not really want to see their corps affected by 'chop and change' political measures. They are not happy when criticized openly, and are hurt by criticism of their work by civilian groups – a feeling which is not confined to the military. To some extent, the non-military environment with its new developments is regarded as a threat.

Here again, we are not making judgements, but simply describing a probable direction of change which has advantages and disadvantages, and is difficult to influence.

This development is probable, but it is not certain, even for the European armed forces. It is still possible that under pressure from politicians or social groupings, or by their own decision, the military will increasingly copy the successful large company management style of the free industrial societies. Several authors have already pointed out that good management need not necessarily differ from good traditional military leadership.[1] However, errors made by a manager in industry seldom have such disastrous effects as those of his military counterpart. This is because the tasks of the two organizations are very different – in industry workers do not have to be ready to risk their lives. Managers may more readily than military commanders choose to act against management principles in the interests of short-term success.

Because of the growing complexity of all decisions and the steadily increasing sums of money involved, the managerial element in the armed forces is growing. Also, during long periods of peace, when no great demands are made on the soldier, the traditional ethics of military leaders tend to be pushed into the background. Terms such as optimism and cost effectiveness gain in significance. But if they lead to superficial management, the group will be destroyed. As regards the group, other values are important.

There is then the danger that the army will break down into individuals each trying to promote his own interests. The individual's career becomes increasingly important; his actions are no longer designed to help the group, but to secure his own promotion. He no longer seeks regimental duty, but prefers to work at headquarters. There is no longer any reason to make sacrifices. He avoids taking risks. Unpleasant jobs which have to be carried out to further his career are done as quickly as possible, without unnecessary exertion.

Besides this, the possibility exists that the growing use of technology will increasingly determine the way of thinking. An almost inevitable consequence would be that the contribution of the individual soldier to the outcome of hostilities would be underestimated.

It is very tempting to subscribe to ideas of superficial management or to a technological outlook. This is because the military leader is required more and more to take purely management decisions, and to obtain an increasingly better understanding of technology. The US forces in Vietnam were in danger of succumbing to this temptation. This will probably increase further as experience of war decreases, as the environment becomes more complex and as technology advances. If one yields to these temptations, motivation in the armed forces will be very quickly destroyed.

The criticism that soldiers always try to create their own little unrealistic world, is made only by those who have not experienced or understood how important a military code of honour is for the performance of a group under heavy pressure. If undervalued or opposed, then an organization which from outside appears to be intact, may be affected internally. At the decisive moment it will not function properly. Even a tendency in this direction should be taken as an indication that serious difficulties lie ahead.

But rather more significant than changes in the range of tasks, and in political and social influences on the armed forces, are changes on the battlefield itself.

We have mentioned that since the end of World War II weapons have greatly improved in range, accuracy of fire, and target effect. Many weapons systems have brought about great savings as regard to weight. This permits an increase in the number of weapons, or at least in the amount of ammunition carried, and this again will lead to even greater effectiveness. Of course compared with nuclear weapons, these increases are minor.

Amongst other measures, it is intended to counter these increases in weapon effectiveness by greater mobility and dispersion. From the point of view of this book this means fighting fire with fire. The increase in weapons' effectiveness will lead to more hits or near misses, and will therefore increase the psychological burden on the soldier. The dispersal together with the increasing emptiness of the battlefield, as well as his greater mobility, will all further his feelings of insecurity.

Because of the increased range and improved accuracy of fire, and the attempt to fight a more mobile battle, the support elements will be more and more involved in the intensive fighting.

In the future the fighting will involve those formations which in World War II had less group cohesion than the front-line troops, and were more readily induced to surrender or to flee when under fire or faced with enemy break-throughs.

Despite improved protective equipment, if nuclear, biological, or chemical weapons are used, the soldier will be put under extra and unaccustomed physical pressures and his fear of mutilation will increase dramatically.

The development and introduction of night vision equipment prevents the soldier from resting and sleeping. Double manning, with relief for exhausted teams, is no answer, since on the battlefield there is never any real rest. It is also questionable whether the reliefs can be integrated into the existing primary groups. It might be better if fully exhausted units were taken out of the fighting together, as often happened in the German army during World War II. Extensive reserves of fresh troops of all types gain added importance and their presence is often decisive.

Looking at it this way, we must ask ourselves again whether the running down of the reserves in favour of front-line troops practised by some NATO armies is sensible. The intention is to be stronger than the enemy in the initial combat, and in this way obtain a quick result, or at least weaken him decisively, but even these tactics can succeed only if at the critical moment in the battle sufficient reserves are available.

The use of night vision aids in mobile warfare could exhaust the soldiers before such a decisive result is obtained. It is conceivable that fully equipped troops not yet involved in the fighting will be exhausted before they see any action. Therefore, decisions concerning numbers of reserves, and, above all, their rest periods will be of much more importance than ever before in deciding the outcome of a battle.

A solid basis for a decision on the number of reserves needed can only be obtained after a close look at the size and tactics of enemy reserves. If initial successes in battle are well publicized they can help to motivate the soldiers. Above all they can be used to advantage by the politicians. But they will rapidly lose their significance, because in a future war everything will be speeded up, including the soldiers' exhaustion.

The advances in technology and the intention to fight a highly mobile battle have repercussions on the commanders. It has been pointed out that leaders are subject to greater physical and psychological stresses than their men. In the future, added to these stresses will be an acceleration of the decision-making process. The ability to fight at night and the means of instant communication will result in no rest for the headquarters staff.

Some of these pressures will be lessened by the use of aids such as data banks and automated displays. But leadership is by nature a creative activity which needs a certain amount of rest. If rest is not granted, decisions and plans become increasingly stereotyped and errors multiply. The commander must withdraw deliberately from the hectic atmosphere and constantly apply himself to objective decision making, on matters such as team work and general assessment of the situation. So his task will become more difficult.

The speeding up of the flow of information may lead commanders at all levels to interfere in the affairs of their subordinates in a similar way to that already described for politicians. It must always be recognized that the delegation of tasks and related responsibilities has two aims: not only that of allowing the commander on the spot to take immediate and independent action, using opportunities which occur only fleetingly in the chaos caused by war, but also ensuring that commanders at all levels retain full responsibility in their own areas of interest. Anybody who interferes risks destroying the mental balance.

Finally, the swifter flow of information may lead to attempts to increase centralization. Staff may be amalgamated, whole levels of command eliminated and units increased in size. Some armed forces have already tried this and have had to reverse some of their decisions. In future battles it will become even more difficult to get a clear picture of the situation — fast transmission of information cannot change this. However, the highly technical weapons systems can only be used to their full effectiveness if the commander is not distracted by too many other tasks. For the future, this will lead to further delegation of tasks and related responsibilities, together with a reduction in the range of those tasks.

The fact that the battle will evolve more rapidly will make it difficult to keep individual soldiers informed of the situation. As a result they will feel increasingly insecure, and their fear of the unknown will mount. The proposal has therefore been made to set up a sort of 'broadcast information service'. It would be technically possible, even if quite expensive; jamming and monitoring by the enemy would bump up the costs. However, it would probably not be very useful, since the information which soldiers really want cannot be broadcast. They want information about their immediate environment, the sort of information that is not available for broadcast during the decisive critical phases of a battle. General statements are of little use.

The continuing technological developments will certainly lead to an increasing diversification of technical aids. Thus modern production plants permit cheaper manufacture of weapons and ammunition which are practically tailor-made for any task. Everything can now be optimized for a particular purpose. These weapons and munitions are not necessarily more complicated to handle and use than their predecessors; the opposite is probably the case. But their increasing variety could lead to over-specialization, which would increase individual soldiers' feelings of insecurity. They must be able to understand what is happening in the area of their vital interests, or they will lose self-confidence. For this reason, either diversification must be limited or the relevant training of all soldiers must be increased.

Advanced technology results in a greater use of armour. Consequently more soldiers are 'locked in' and cannot relieve the pressures by bodily activity.

It is probable that weapons-handling will be simplified, which means that the physical disadvantages arising from the stress situation itself (nervousness, fear, trembling) can be reduced without the need to take drugs. However, this again leads to a greater accuracy of fire, and hence to an increased stress on everyone − it is a vicious circle.

Dependence on technology and technologists will increase. In World War II it was often possible for a soldier to fight the enemy with comparatively simple weapons such as rifles, hand grenades and mines. Such methods of combat will only occasionally have a place in the age of laser beams, night vision equipment and chemical weapons. As a result war will become less personal and perhaps, because of this, easier to bear. However, it means that high morale will often only be of value if supported by appropriate technological means.

The soldier of the future will come from a different background. Not only are standards of living rising but urbanization is increasing. To assess the consequences of this is difficult; however, it seems clear that the capacity to withstand pressures will not increase. Education will be improved further, and, above all, the individual will specialize more and more. He will no longer understand the increasingly complex world and may therefore, especially in his younger years, often unreflectingly accept fashionable opinions and defend them vigorously. The significance of many concepts such as 'family', 'motherland', 'honour' or 'freedom' could be changed entirely within a short time. As regards the horrors to be anticipated in a future war, the catchword 'Better red than dead' might hold a new attraction.

Armed forces, particularly those relying on national service, are very quickly and constantly exposed to these swings in outlook, and this will put strains on the relationship between the older professional soldiers and the younger national servicemen.

This general trend will probably strengthen the desire to form groupings. Such a desire can be made use of by the forces, but it can also encourage real or fashion-following conflicts of conscience which can make it increasingly difficult to assess the operational value of national servicemen, and especially of reservists.

Father figures of all sorts will probably continue to gain influence, and this should also be of benefit to the forces.

However, taken together, all these trends will affect military formations less than the rest of society.

A surprise outbreak of war would not give the soldiers time to prepare gradually for the horrors already described, so pressures would increase. A surprise outbreak cannot be entirely ruled out, despite the continual improvements in reconnaissance aids and stronger ties between countries, though it seems less likely now. This is perhaps the only area where future developments could improve the soldier's lot.

Does the use of nuclear weapons result only in another form of death? Should one expect the front-line soldier to bear greater hardship and suffering? If one studies the gloomy forecasts on future wars, and investigates their probability, then one must come to the conclusion that, even for the hard-pressed front-line soldier, the future looks worse than the past. Both commanders and their men are likely to be physically and psychologically exhausted within a few days or at the most several weeks. This is because of the emptiness of the battlefield, the mobility, the higher number of deaths, wounded, and near-misses, nuclear, biological and chemical weapons, and the ability to fight at night.

However, the effect on all types of support troops will be even greater. They will be increasingly subjected to the same horrors as the front-line soldiers, and must learn to resist them.

The people back home will no longer give the soldiers the same unequivocal backing as in previous wars. The diversity of tasks will increase.

All this may face men who have become used to an increasingly liberal life-style, lived according to individual interests and free from serious worries regarding their basic needs. This underlines the significance of the measures described in this book. It will be even more important to follow them in future.

Hitherto we have assumed that in a future armed conflict together with all its horrors, social conventions would still be observed. This may not be so, and everything laid down in agreements, written and unwritten, may be ignored by irresponsible leaders bent on total war.

This possibility is by no means far-fetched. In the last analysis the threat to use nuclear weapons is not easily reconciled with the ethics of our society. Many of these rules were broken only recently in Indochina. Why should the step in this direction not be taken further?

One would like to avoid this consideration of the future, because many of the factors examined are unimaginable. But we must face facts, because there may be a time in the future when it will be necessary to change even fundamental tactics in order to reduce unbearable pressures on the soldier. It may, for example, become necessary to restrict mobility and thereby give the soldier and his group the feeling of secure integration in a solid and indestructible system.

The soldiers of NATO have at least one advantage. Their aim is defence. It is true that defence cannot be mounted without counter-attacking, but the defender has an overall psychological advantage over the attacker. Perhaps this advantage can be exploited more successfully than hitherto by increased preparation in peace-time. Factors that should be considered are: knowledge of the terrain, cover, demolition, obstacles, deployment in depth, reconnaissance systems, organization of relief, deception, ambushes and tank-traps. Perhaps the advantages can be used to such an extent that after a short while they will demoralize any attacker. They might even deter him from armed conflict — that is if the political deterrent of nuclear weapons should lose some of its impact.

Every army is in danger of preparing itself for the last war. This need not be a disadvantage, as long as no major technical developments have occurred. But the weapons systems which have been, or are about to be introduced into service, have nothing in common with those used in World War II. Their quality has changed in such a way that they will have a new and considerable impact on each soldier. Therefore, it is worthwhile considering whether tactics should be changed accordingly – for the West German Army at least has not undergone any major adaptations since the last days of World War II. Man's performance cannot be increased further. In the future it is he who will continue to decide the outcome of the battle. Thus all enquiries into possible changes in fundamental tactics must have him in mind.

NOTE

1. E. Dinter, *Führungslehre*.

CHAPTER SIXTEEN

Open Questions

It was pointed out earlier that the purpose of war and combat is to force a reluctant adversary to submit to one's own will by the use of brute force. Other chapters have also made clear that success or failure in battle depends above all on the front-line fighter. Therefore, armed forces, when deciding on personnel selection, organization, or weapons development, must take into consideration his probable behaviour.

It is disconcerting for these policy-makers to find that there are many published opinions on the subject, but that the scientific studies supporting or disproving them are hidden in archives and can often be brought to light only after a long and hard search. They exist in surprisingly great numbers and their quality in most cases cannot be doubted. Nevertheless they are ignored.

This leads to the first task to be undertaken in the future — a competent team of doctors, psychologists, sociologists, forecasters, historians and soldiers must collect and collate the existing scientific literature. If possible they should be attached to an institution of the armed forces which is concerned with the behaviour of soldiers such as the 'Centre for Leadership and Civic Education' of the West German Armed Forces.

Collection and collation will be a lengthy process. Personnel changes should be avoided as much as possible. Peter Watson has taken a first step in this direction.[1] This team will find, as the author did when researching the present book, that practically all important aspects of the behaviour of the fighting man have been studied already.

Thus in writing this book, it was decided not to dilute its basic concept by bringing together all of the many findings which were discovered. This called for self-discipline. It would have been attractive to detail the importance of good care for the wounded, and to consider the relationship of the soldier to his equipment, the dangers of rapid success in battle (the advantages have been discussed), humour, self-mutilation, the fear of imprisonment, psychosomatic illness, and behaviour during captivity, the relationship between front-line soldiers and others, the effects of organizational or supply difficulties on motivation, welfare matters, the effects on future soldiers of the treatment of those demobilized after war, or even 'class warfare' and motivation for defence. The answers to all these questions have been given elsewhere.

New objective investigations should only be undertaken if the available material has been thoroughly assessed. These investigations could later be entrusted to the same team which has to make the assessment. Cooperation in NATO should be attempted, since it is to be hoped that fewer and fewer soldiers will have the necessary battle experience to enable them to give the researchers the required answers. It is also a question of finance. Field investigations in particular are expensive. It would be worthwhile cooperating closely with the USA, which has already invested a great deal of time and money in such research programmes, and is one of the leading nations in this field.

A second future task will be to refine the procedures and methods already used. Personnel selection is paramount. The personality traits demanded of the soldier and his commanders cannot be taught to the young man in the forces. They can be revealed and encouraged only if they are already present, and this depends on inheritance and education, factors on which the forces can have little or no influence.

This book has made clear that the leaders and the led may possess two completely different personality structures. It has shown in particular that there are 'fighters' and 'passengers'. All fighting forces devote much attention to the selection of the leaders. They have some success. In the ranks also, those clearly psychologically unfit to bear pressures are exempted from service or are rejected. But there is still considerable scope for improvement.

It has been shown, by the few historical examples included in this book, that the situations which a soldier may face in battle are so varied and so extreme that it is practically impossible to foresee in peace-time who will be able to cope. A certain number of errors must be accepted. Nevertheless, this number should be reduced. It is not only necessary to examine all potential soldiers before enlistment. They must also be assessed after they have joined. This is rarely done. A method should be found for re-posting or discharging soldiers who, for example, show weak nerves during any part of their service. If soldiers engaged in parachute jumping, throwing hand grenades, firing anti-tank weapons, or abseiling refuse to do so in peace-time, then they will certainly refuse in battle. These peace-time tasks are ideal hurdles which will be faced in training. There is no need to set them up specially. It is worthwhile assessing the soldier objectively throughout his training.

This raises problems, in particular for armed forces which depend on national service. These problems are even greater if those psychologically unable to bear the pressures are thrown into the horrors of battle. Nobody should be carelessly exposed to them. Furthermore, careful personnel selection can do nothing but good for the reputation of the forces.

Over-selective personnel recruitment could make it difficult for volunteer armies to meet target figures. Discharge of unsuitable personnel might lead to legal difficulties.

With volunteers it would be helpful to make a wide survey on why young men wish to serve in the armed forces or are prepared to assume the burdens of command. Such information would be important in formulating a recruitment policy. Thus, young men with definite weaknesses could feel attracted by the clear hierarchical, and at the same time welfare-orientated structure of the armed forces. In the chaos of battle, this sort of man might not retain his strength of will to carry on and might fail to take an active part in the fighting.

Thus human or male aggressiveness could be a motivation for service, but this has not yet been demonstrated. Such investigations would make it easier to exclude unsuitable applicants. Here again the search for quality is an advantage not only to the armed forces in general, but also to the individual soldier.

It has been stated that only a few are able to fight on their own with their individual weapons, and that the rest can be integrated into the activities of a team. Therefore, it is important to find out who belongs to which type so that each can be used for appropriate tasks.

No study has been found which gives even an approximate indication of the optimum mix of 'fighters' and 'passengers'. To have too many 'fighters' in one group could be just as bad as having too few.

Third, there are some matters which merit study because, though they may not be relevant to our own forces, they may be of significance in enabling judgments to be made about the behaviour of other armed forces. These include the whole field of the use of drugs, or the possibility of 'pre-stressing' or 'pre-conditioning' soldiers before they see action.

Finally, there are some areas which, although not of the utmost importance, should be considered, because it may be possible to reach new and important conclusions.

Panic was not studied in this book, because the author was unable to find any references in the literature. This may have been due either to wrong defintion or to lack of persistence.

The author has said nothing about looting, which was one of the main motives for fighting in earlier centuries. Nor has he discussed the sexual behaviour of soldiers. This may be due to the author's inhibitions.

Nothing has been said about the ideal age of a commander or his men. This may be because in urgent war situations nobody had any choice and therefore did not worry about it.

All these points are worthy of further consideration.

However, any further research should be preceded by a comprehensive survey in order to select the most crucial from among the large range of possible topics. Crucial topics should certainly include personnel selection. Even apparently marginal areas cannot be entirely neglected, since they may give clues about the behaviour of a potential enemy – and possibly also new insights into one's own problems.

NOTE

1. P. Watson, *War on the Mind*.

CHAPTER SEVENTEEN

Conclusion

The intention of this book was to omit as far as possible any aspect not directly related to psychology, sociology, or the military profession. But as the work progressed, it very quickly became clear, as the reader may have found, that this was practically impossible.

The many individual stories reflect the brutality of war and the resultant extreme needs of the soldier in such a horrifying way that one would prefer to ignore them.

The scientific literature analyses this distress. Seemingly without feeling, it describes the aggressiveness, ideology, the fight for power, desire for money or fame, and the spirit of adventure of aggressors and victims alike. In the end the findings of this book, obtained by research and backed by logic, appear even more heartless and inhuman. Anybody who was not already horrified by the personal accounts and the scientific studies, must in the end feel sickened by the conclusions of this book. Does it not suggest that man is only an animal and can be easily manipulated? Does it not try to find out only how the soldier can tolerate even more inhumanity, so that all, friend or foe alike, will head for disaster even more quickly?

No, this is not at all the conclusion to be drawn. Rather the opposite is true. During the research for this book it became clear that man can inflict terrible horrors on his fellows without too many scruples. The author was shaken by this, and considered omitting them. It became obvious why the specialist literature gives so many differing answers to the central questions. The truth seemed to be in conflict with our social conventions.

The author was not only wary of airing disagreeable and dissentient views. He was also concerned about publishing information which might be misused by people without any respect for human lives. When the study began it was like observing the genie in the bottle in the fairy tale. The author was driven on by curiosity, seeking to explore its powers. To do this, he had to release it from its prison.

Once its frightening powers revealed themselves he wished it back in the bottle again. Scientists have in the past often made discoveries thought beneficial to society, yet which have sometimes resulted in the production of weapons which have increased the misery and suffering of soldiers and civilians. When faced with these thoughts, the author was tempted to give up.

For a time, the work came to a standstill. The author tried to put this theme to the back of his mind. He very nearly decided to give up his study of the pressures on the soldier in battle, and to write instead a concise and easy-to-read book on the psychology of leadership in peace-time.

Then however, it became clear to him that if he suppressed the publication of this knowledge further horrors might occur. On superficial examination it seems as though in times of the greatest physical and psychological pressures only the animal in man survives. However, it becomes clear on closer consideration that educational and cultural influences considerably determine our behaviour even in such extreme situations. If the findings of this book seem to be heartless and dispel some of our illusions, they do give advice on how man can and must be made responsible for the way he reacts, even in a crisis.

Therefore this book is addressed directly to three main groups: political leaders, the responsibly-minded public, and the soldier himself, whether he issues orders or obeys them.

Deep down, this is a pacifist book, but in a realistic way. It shows continuously what war means, and makes it clear once more to the political leader in power that he must devote all his energy to avoiding it. It is clear to those who understand psychology, sociology, and politics that war can be delayed for long periods, but cannot be prevented for ever. Only the naive believe that it can be. Consequently, the realist must be ready for war and prepare himself for it. And here lies a second obligation for government. It must in the event of war endeavour to reduce the horrors, in the spirit of the Geneva Convention.

Finally, the political leadership in war, knowing that the aim is to force the enemy to yield, not necessarily to destroy him, must avoid senseless sacrifices. The suffering of the individual, described in the early chapters of this book, must be kept in mind when making political decisions.

But the book is also addressed to the public. We all carry our share of responsibility for the horrors of a possible future war. We must all support or actively encourage a sensible avoidance of war, a humanization of war, and ensure that the politicians conduct the war responsibly.

We must all be aware that we influence potential fighters. We do this in the way we educate our children and form their character, and by the way we behave in private and in public. The soldiers in Calais, Stalingrad and Cassino in their dire situations were largely controlled by their atavistic needs, but their ethics depended on how they had been influenced by their family, friends, schools and clubs.

Finally, this book is addressed to soldiers. Commanders at all levels have the duty to prepare the soldiers entrusted to them for the terrors of a possible war. Without the courageous action of every soldier a nation cannot exist in freedom. This book makes a great number of suggestions for his preparation for battle, but only commanders can put them into practice. In peacetime it will not always be easy to apply them.

Therefore, the ethics of our society cannot be ignored. Our ideas of human dignity forbid for example that soldiers should be given intoxicants such as alcohol before commencing an attack, so that they can better control their fears. But they do not prevent us accepting as recruits only those who are the most likely to withstand both the physical and psychological pressures of war without ill effects.

Thus there is demanded of the military leader not only a pure technical weaponry decision, but also an ethical one.

For the individual soldier in action, this book shows that even in a crisis he can be made morally responsible for all his actions. Many wrong reactions are understandable, but they cannot be condoned.

The book has shown that man cannot be manipulated fundamentally. This is comforting. We may not like a particular human reaction, either for practical or ethical reasons. Nevertheless, the dominance of inheritance, upbringing, education and basic needs will continue. Therefore, we can always expect a consistent and pre-determined behaviour. If the reverse were the case, if intellectual thought was dominant, man could easily become the tool of the tyrant.

Thus this book is more than a cold-blooded analysis of the behaviour of the soldier in war. The author has tried to avoid ethical considerations and has not given answers in this decisive area. But the examples show that answers are required. Each reader has to find his own. He must take it a step further than this book.

Selected Bibliography

Böhmler, R., *Monte Cassino* (Cassell, 1964).
   Contains many personal stories.

Connell, C., *Monte Cassino* (Elek, 1963).
   Contains many individual accounts mainly from the Polish viewpoint.

Craig, W., *Enemy at the Gates: the Battle for Stalingrad* (Hodder & Stoughton, 1973).
   Not entirely objective but there are numerous individual anecdotes.

Dinter, E., *Führungslehre – Arbeitsmaximen und Arbeitstechniken für die Praxis* (Bonn, Mittler & Sohn, 1980).
   Basic rules for the peacetime commander.

Dixon, N. F., *On the Psychology of Military Incompetence* (Cape, 1976).
   A wide-ranging study giving many historical examples of how genetics and upbringing influence the behaviour of leaders.

Freud, S., 'Warum Krieg?' *Gesammelte Schriften* vol. 12 (1932).
   The statements on death and killing are as relevant now as they were when written.

Freud, S., 'Zeitgemässes über Krieg und Tod', *Gesammelte Schriften* vol. 10 (1924).

Hastings, R., *The Rifle Brigade* (Gale and Polden Ltd., 1950).

Janovitz, M., *Military Conflict-Essays in the Institutional Analysis of War and Peace* (Sage, 1975).
   A collection of lectures and articles. The paper on group cohesion was used by the author in the preparation of this book.

Kehrig, M., *Stalingrad* (Deutsche Verlags-Anstalten, Stuttgart 1974).
   A comprehensive scientific study, in German.

Majdalany, F., *Cassino* (Longman, 1957).
   A comprehensive account from the British and Allied viewpoints containing many eye-witness accounts.

Majdalany, F., *The Monastery* 4th edn. (John Lane / The Bodley Head, 1950).
   An absorbing account of the battle for Cassino written by a participant.

Marshall, S. L. A., *Men against Fire* (William Morrow, New York 1947).
   This study stresses the importance of the infantry, and describes

particularly the relationship between and the motivation of fighting and non-combatant troops.

Neave, A., *The Flames of Calais* (Hodder & Stoughton, 1977).
The author participated in the battle for Calais and uses many personal accounts.

Noyce, W., *They Survived: a Study of the Will to Live* (Heinemann, 1962).

Office of the Surgeon General, Department of the Army, *Neuropsychiatry in World War II* (Washington, 1966, 1973).
Describes the history of neuropsychiatry in the American Army in World War II and the Korean War. The statistical information is particularly interesting.

Schröter, H., *Stalingrad* (Eduard Kaiser Verlag, no date).
The author was at Stalingrad. It is of more interest for the eye-witness account than for its historical value. In German.

Stouffer, S. A., *et al. The American Soldier*, 4 volumes (Princeton University Press, Princeton, USA, 1949).
A comprehensive statistical approach showing how soldiers adapt to life in the forces. It describes their behaviour before and during battle. Volume 2 in particular includes information on the behaviour of soldiers in action.

Swank, R. L. and Marchand, W. E., 'Combat Neurosis: Development of Combat Exhaustion', *Archives of Neurology and Psychiatry* vol. 55 (1946).
A short article outlining the pressures which soldiers face in battle.

von Plehwe, F. K., *Reiter, Streiter und Rebell* (Schäuble Verlag, 1976).
A biography of Lieutenant-General Baade who took part in the battle for Stalingrad as Commander of the 90th Armoured Infantry Division.

War Office 'Report of the War Office Committee of Enquiry into shellshock' (HMSO, 1922).
A wide ranging investigation into psychiatric casualties in the British army during World War 1.

Watson, P., *War on the Mind – The Military Uses and Abuses of Psychology* (Hutchinson, London, 1978).
An analytical listing of psychological studies relating to the behaviour of soldiers in battle.

Background Reading

Ahrenfeld, R. H., *Psychiatry in the British Army in the Second World War* (Routledge & Kegan Paul, London, 1958).
A historical study which gives a good description of the problems of training soldiers and of their motivation.

Baylis, *et al. Contemporary Strategy – Theories and Policies* (Croom Helm,

London, 1975).
A summary of defence policy and strategies of the world powers.

Bidwell, S., *Modern Warfare – a study of Men, Weapons, and Theories* (Allen Lane, London, 1973).
A study of future developments in the conduct of war.

Bigler, R. R., *Der einsame Soldat* (Verlag Huber & Co., Frauenfeld (Schweiz), 1963).
A book which calls for the use of 'directives', cooperative leadership and observance of group dynamics. It gives little information not provided already in the books by Marshall.

Eibl-Elbesfeld, I., *Krieg und Frieden aus der Sicht der Verhaltenforschung* (Piper & Co., München, Zürich, 1975).

Ellis, J., *The Sharp End of War – The Fighting Man in World War II* (David & Charles, London, 1980).
A description worth reading of the pressures on soldiers in war. It is based on individual stories and on statistics. It is not very systematic and no conclusions are drawn.

Franzen, E., *Testpsychologie – Persönlichkeits- und Charaktertest* 10th edn. (Ullstein Bücher, Nr. 181, Frankfurt/M., Berlin, 1969).

Gabriel, R. A. and Savage, P. L., *Crisis in Command – Mismanagement in the Army* (Hill and Wang, New York, 1978).
A study of the reasons for the 'failure' of the US forces in Vietnam.

Güggenbühl, *et al. Truppenpsychologie* (Verlag Huber, Frauenfeld (Schweiz), 1978).
The title is rather misleading, as this book is only a collection of individual studies and unfortunately gives no overall picture.

Janowitz, M., *The Professional Soldier, a Social and Political Portrait* Library of Congress Catalogue Card No. 60-7090 (The Free Press of Glencoe, Illinois, 1960).
A comprehensive study of the US Forces, worth reading.

König, R., (ed.) *Beiträge zur Militärsoziologie* (Westdeutscher Verlag, Köln und Opladen, 1968).
Particularly worth reading in this book are the articles on 'Self-interests, Primary Groups and Ideology' and on 'Leadership in the Military'. It contains a good bibliography.

Kontakte (Prof. Dr. Bastian H.O.), *Militärische Menschenführung in Kleinen Gruppen* (Ausbildungshilfe der Schule der Bundeswehr für Innere Führung – now: Zentrum Innere Führung – Bundesministerium der Verteidigung, Bonn, 1979).

Karobejnikov/Scheltov, *Soldat und Krieg – Probleme der moralisch-politologischen und psychologischen Vorbereitung in der Sowjetarmee* (Militärverlag der Deutschen Democratischen Republik, Berlin, 1973).

The latest in a series of five books. Most of them have been written by the same Russian authors. They have been published since 1957 also in the GDR. The content is fairly undemanding. The number of these publications underlines the importance which is given to psychology in the Warsaw Pact Forces.

Lippert, E., *Mädchen unter Waffen − Gesellschafts- und sozialpolitische Aspekte weiblicher Soldaten* ISBN 3 7890 0621 1 (Nomos Verlagsgesellschaft, Baden Baden, 1980).

Marshall, S. L. A., *Pork Chop Hill − The American Fighting Man in Action, Korea, Spring 1953* Library of Congress Catalogue Card No. 56 9546 (William Morrow and Company, New York, 1956).
Another work by Marshall. Its detailed stories of the fighting of sections and platoons give important conclusions on the pressures and behaviour of soldiers in battle, well worth reading.

Miksche, F. O., *Atomic Weapons and Armies* (Faber and Faber Ltd., London, not dated, probably 1955).
The effect of atomic weapons on the tactics of the future.

Moran, Lord, *The Anatomy of Courage* (Constable, London, 1945).

Richardson, F. M., *Fighting Spirit − Psychological Factors in War* (Leo Cooper, London, 1978).
The last two books are typical examples of the analysis of pressures written by experienced participants in war. The many arguments and questions arouse interest, but because they are not founded on any systematic scientific basis, they make some mistaken recommendations.

'Panic: Erkennen − Verhüten − Bekämpfen', Schriftenreihe *Innere Führung* Reihe Erziehung − Heft 8 − 2. Auflage, Bundesministerium der Verteidigung, FüB I − FüB 14 (June 1963).
Well worth reading. 'Panic' is also defined as 'desperado behaviour' of the individual. This is contrary to the assumptions made in this book.

Poggeler, F., *Der Mensch in Mündigkeit und Reife − Eine Anthropologie des Erwachsenen*, 2nd edn. (Ferdinand Schöningh, Paderborn, 1970).

Rolbant, S., *The Israeli Soldier − Profile of an Army*, ISBN 498 074889 (South Brunswick, Thomas Yoseloff, New York, London, 1970).
A sociological study of the Israeli Armed Forces.

Schneider, W., *Das Buch vom Soldaten*, 1st edn. (Econ Verlag, Düsseldorf, Wien, 1964).
A broad description of the behaviour of soldiers over the centuries − interesting because of the large number of traditional ideas and historical examples. It is of literary rather than scientific value. No conclusions are reached.

Introduction to the Historical Examples

The author's intention is to give as broad a picture as possible of the experiences of combatants. He uses as examples accounts by soldiers in the most varied battle conditions. These have already been authenticated and evaluated with much effort by historians. In no case was the selection of books determined by their other qualities.

In order to achieve a certain comparison of historical events with possible future wars in Central Europe, reference was made only to World War II in Europe. Nevertheless, World War I, which imposed extreme pressures on the soldiers involved in trench warfare, would have been eminently suitable, as would the Arab-Israeli wars because of the use of modern weapons.

Two longer battles (Stalingrad and Cassino) and a shorter one (Calais) were chosen in order to establish whether the duration of a battle has any fundamental effect on the behaviour of the participants.

Although all arms of the services are subjected to similar pressures, this investigation has been concerned exclusively with the land forces. This is partly because there is a large amount of useful information available describing soldiers in action, but also because large numbers of them were submitted to great pressures for extended periods rather more often than their comrades in the naval or air forces. These extreme situations are the most informative for a study of this kind. However, the conclusions in the main text can be applied unreservedly to all arms.

Observations from the British side have assumed a certain preponderance. This is because the available sources are particularly numerous and tend especially to concentrate upon the position of the individual soldier, the small fighting unit and commanders at the lowest level.

Books by historians with extensive personal experience of war were particularly useful. They found analysis and assessment of wartime experiences relatively easy. But the most valuable were the statements made by the soldiers themselves, especially when they were made spontaneously or without much forethought.

Most of the statements made by historians and eye witnesses alike serve to establish historical truth rather than to investigate the physical and psychological pressures on the soldier in battle. This actually proved to be an advantage. Although terms such as 'panic' or 'shock' were often applied wrongly, the choice of words, uninfluenced by psychology or sociology, offers the expert a deep insight. For instance, the premature and precipitate destruction of weapons to prevent them falling into enemy hands is an excellent example of the conflict between fear and group morale. This is described in a regimental history which would have preferred to remain silent on the matter.

A large number of documents were examined, but in the end an attempt was made to compile the extracts, which provide typical examples of important experiences, from as few sources as possible. It is hoped that this will open up the possibility of a purposeful study for the reader interested in history. The number of extracts from each source has been restricted. This was possible where the same or similar circumstances were described, but was done only reluctantly, as many accounts are exciting and worth reading. However, the author was aware that too large a book would attract only a few readers.

In order to facilitate reading and subsequent analysis, the experiences are arranged in seven overlapping groups. They are: general pressures; pressures on the individual; injury and death; stamina and exhaustion; firepower; experiences of units; experiences of leaders. In addition, most extracts are provided with a comment in brackets which gives a reference to the evaluation in the main text. A note of the source is given at the end of the examples. The author's explanatory notes appear in brackets.

For the reader in a hurry who may have extensive battle experience it may suffice to read the extracts of one battle only, possibly the one he is most familiar with. The investigations of the other battles provide no new information. They serve more for a brief comparative review, although there are a number of interesting additions in each.

ACKNOWLEDGEMENTS

Extracts from William Craig: *Enemy at the Gates* are reprinted by permission of the Harold Matson Company Inc; from Fred Majdalaney, *The Monastery* and *Cassino* by permission of the estate of the late Fred Majdalany; from Airey Neave, *The Flames of Calais* by permission of Curtis Brown Ltd, London on behalf of the estate of Airey Neave; from Rudolph Böhmler, *Monte Cassino* by permission of the Macmillan Publishing Company; from Charles Connell, *Monte Cassino* by permission of Granada Publishing Ltd.

The Battle for Calais

BACKGROUND

On 1 September 1939 Germany invaded Poland. Poland's security had been guaranteed previously by Great Britain and France, and they declared war on Germany on 3 September 1939.

On 10 May 1940, after having occupied Denmark and Norway, Germany attacked the west. Two armoured corps, commanded by Guderian and Hoth, broke through the defences of the Western Allies, continued their advance through the Ardennes which had been considered impassable, and as early as 20 May reached the Channel coast at Noyelles.

On 21 May the British Expeditionary Force (BEF) mounted a counter-attack at Arras. It was repulsed, but it reinforced the uneasy feeling which the Germans had regarding their long and unprotected flanks. Probably it resulted also in Hitler's order to Guderian to halt the advance at the Somme. As a result, time was gained to prepare the defence of the Channel ports, which in the end made possible the successful evacuation of 330,000 officers, NCOs and soldiers of the BEF and their Allies from Dunkirk.

THE BATTLE

The defence of Calais was important for the evacuation from Dunkirk, as Calais provided cover for Dunkirk from the south, and in addition, it tied down enemy forces which would otherwise have been available for operations directly against the BEF.

On 22 May the Third Royal Tank Regiment (3 RTR) and the Queen Victoria's Rifles (QVR) disembarked and immediately took up the defence of the suburbs of Calais.

On 23 May the King's Royal Rifle Corps (60th Rifles) and the 1st Battalion, the Rifle Brigade accompanied by an additional anti-tank company arrived and stiffened the defence.

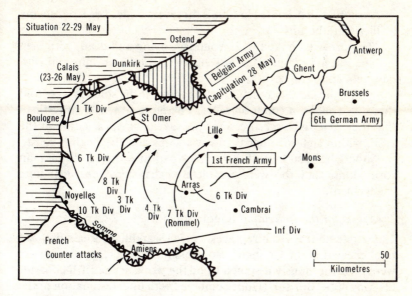

Situation 22-29 May

Ostend
Calais (23-26 May) — Dunkirk
Antwerp
Belgian Army (Capitulation 28 May)
Ghent
Brussels
6th German Army
1 Tk Div
Boulogne
St Omer
Lille
6 Tk Div
1st French Army
Mons
8 Tk Div
Arras
Noyelles 3 Tk Div
6 Tk Div
10 Tk Div 4 Tk Div 7 Tk Div (Rommel)
Cambrai
Inf Div
Somme
French Counter attacks
Amiens
0   50
Kilometres

These four units of battalion strength, together with parts of the Searchlight Regiment and some 800 Frenchmen, and a not inconsiderable number of volunteers of very differing origin (altogether their strength was about 4000), defended Calais against the ten German Armoured Divisions for four days and nights. On 26 May the survivors of this small fighting force had to surrender and were taken prisoner.

On 4 June the evacuation from Dunkirk was concluded successfully.

PRESSURES

General Pressures (author's summary)

The British units and formations deployed had no recent battle experience. Some of them included a high proportion of reservists.

All were thrown into the battle hastily and without preparation of any kind.

They, like the attackers, had to fight in a foreign country.

In the confusion caused by the rapid German advance, they received contradictory and sometimes nonsensical orders.

They were equipped quite inadequately, had no artillery of their own and not even the necessary ammunition.

As soon as they landed in Calais they were under fire from enemy artillery and bombs.

The port was choked with wounded, dying and dead, with men who had been ordered back or separated from their units and with deserters and refugees.

During the last 24 hours of the engagement the soldiers were told that they could not count on relief. Therefore, it was clear to them that they were to be sacrificed for the sake of the evacuation of the BEF, within sight of their British warships and the English coast.

Although the success of their attack had encouraged the German formations, they too were completely exhausted from their long engagement.

Pressures on the Individual (Quotations)

1. Despite alarms from refugees ... we [Searchlight Regiment] did not believe that the Germans had broken through ... such rumours were contemptuously assumed to be the work of the fifth column. (21 May 40 − British). (Hope combined with underestimation of the enemy).

2. I [Lt Neave] was not greatly alarmed. I could not believe that, despite all the confusion, the British High Command would be so ill-informed. (22 May − British). (Hope).

3. By 7.30 a.m. the news that evacuation had been decided 'in principle' had become known to most British troops in Calais and many breathed a sigh of relief. (24 May − British). (Hope).

4. As we [Searchlight Regiment] approached the medieval town of Ardres, ten miles south of Calais, a woman spat at us and called us cowards. She shook her fist and shouted: 'Merde!' This did not impress us in the least ... (21 May − British). (Group cohesion with disdain for others, in this case foreigners).

5. ... the roads round Calais were choked with refugees making for the coast. But to the Searchlight men who did not speak French, the 'panic' was thought unnecessary, hysterical and ridiculous. (21 May − British). (Group cohesion and group morale).

6. British and French leaders now took refuge in the expression 'Allied solidarity' which appears in numerous directives and telegrams. It meant very little to the troops or their commanders and it

was differently interpreted by the two governments. (May 1940 – British). (Group cohesion with a contempt for others).

7. At this point the driver was hit and the lorry stopped ... The wounded who could move, began to crawl towards them. Edward Bird ran across the road, climbed into the driver's seat under tremendous machine-gun fire and tried to restart the lorry. There were still several gravely wounded men in the back. But he was shot in the head and staggered back, to die in half an hour. (25 May – British). (Group cohesion and the desire for approval).

8. About 7 p.m. ... At the Pont Faidherbe ..., three tanks began to cross followed by a saloon car. One tank forced the road-block but was put out of action. The second was also hit and stopped. The third withdrew to cheers from the riflemen. (25 May – British). (Group cohesion and success).

9. Save for the occasional shell which landed in the harbour area, the night had been quiet. But it had been impossible to sleep so strong was the sense of danger. By now, I [Lt Neave] knew that Calais would soon be surrounded. I realised that there would be a bloody battle. (23/24 May – British). (Fear while waiting for the engagement).

10. ... Colonel Keller [CO of the 3 RTR] was told by Nicholson [Commander of Calais] that men not required for tank crews could leave on the *Kohistan*.
    'Orders were issued', wrote Colonel Holland after the war, 'that tanks and transport likely to fall intact into enemy hands were to be destroyed. Owing to a misunderstanding some tanks were prematurely destroyed.' ... many believed that evacuation was actually about to take place. (24 May – British). (Fear and an attempt at 'honourable' surrender).

11. Early in the morning an artillery duel began between the Tenth Panzer Division's guns on the high ground at Coquelles and the coastal guns ... of Fort Lapin, the Bastion de l'Estran and Bastion 2. These batteries were enthusiastic and prodigal of ammunition. By 10 a.m. the Bastion de l'Estran had fired 683 rounds out of a stock of 895. A Rifle Brigade officer observed that the main idea of the French gunners 'was to get rid of their ammunition as quickly as possible'. There was too much truth in this remark for comfort.

(24 May — British). (Fear, group morale and the attempt at an 'honourable' surrender).

12. Since the 23rd [of May], snipers had been active in all parts of Calais, and they had been concealed in the town for some days. Since the effect of a fifth column is partly psychological, it is possible to exaggerate their numbers. (24 May — British). (Fear of the unknown).

13. My [Lt Neave] immediate fear was that the Germans would break through in the next few minutes, that I [being wounded] should be left behind and captured. It was a fear shared by all. We had a confused but horrific picture of what awaited us if we were taken prisoner by the Nazis. Death in action was something everyone faced, but stories of the ill-treatment of prisoners, of concentration camps, made capture seem the worst of all. (24 May — British). (Fear of the unknown).

14. At the Cellulose Factory, shells burst in the yard and yellow acrid smoke drifted towards the ramparts. There was a cry of 'Gas!' and respirators were hurriedly put on until a few minutes afterwards it became clear that the smoke was only cordite. Several gas alarms occurred in other parts of Calais during the 25th May, all of them false. (British). (Fear of the unknown and the unexpected).

15. Lying half-unconscious on my bloodstained stretcher in the tunnel, I [Lt Neave] saw the shadow of a large figure in German uniform leaning over me. I remember now most vividly the sense of peace after the shattering roar of the battle. (26 May — British). (Fear and relief from fear).

16. In the tunnel under Bastion I, a young soldier blew his brains out rather than surrender. (26 May — British). (Group cohesion, exhaustion with despair, fear of the unknown).

17. Inside [Bastion 2], men ... had been busy trying to mend the coastal guns spiked by the French garrison on the previous day. One gun was repaired, turned inland and fired at a German tank. There was a tremendous bang and the barrel rolled off into the sand. A roar of laughter from the Q.V.R. rose along the northern rampart. (25 May — British). (Group cohesion and humour).

18. Afterwards I heard them [Churchill's comments on the battle of Calais, which he made to the House of Commons on 5 June 1940]

on a secret radio ... A defenceless prisoner across the Channel, I felt in my desolation that I was near to home and not forgotten. (1940 – British). (Ties with the people back home).

Injury and Death (Quotations)

19. The 24th May was spent [by the Rifle Brigade] 'in manoeuvre' against the 69th German Rifle Regiment ... Some witnesses describe a 'holiday spirit'. Riflemen shot at the Germans as if it was 'glorified rabbit shooting' in which they were engaged. (British). (No fear of killing or of one's own death, group morale).

20. Dispatch riders tested whether streets were under fire by riding up and down and reporting them safe 'provided you went fast enough'. Many of the men kept these youthful high spirits until, surrounded and outnumbered, they were forced to surrender. But the older men were more serious. (24 May – British). (Group morale and the desire for approval overcomes the fear of injury and death).

21. When I [Lt Neave] came to, I was lying on the pavement, still afraid of being taken prisoner. I urged the medical orderly to get me out of the line but he was inclined to talk professionally about the condition of the wound. He was certain I had been shot through the lung. I swore at him and ordered him to help me into the next street. A Frenchman joined us, young and talkative, and slowly they walked me away. (24 May – British). (Fear and hope of release from the fear).

22. I [Lt Neave] was suffering more from anger than pain. No one seemed to know the way to the 60th regimental aid post ... My chief interest was in evacuation by sea to England. (24 May – British). (Fear and hope of release from fear).

23. At eight o'clock Peter Brush was shot through the throat by a sniper, but refused to leave his headquarters ... At ten o'clock John Taylor arrived with orders to send Peter Brush to the regimental aid post. (25 May – British). (Group cohesion with a desire for approval).

24. Brush had again been wounded, and he was wounded a third time before it was all over. Peel and 2/Lieut. Surtees, though unable to move from severe leg wounds, kept firing till the Germans appeared on the skyline and took them prisoner. With them was Rifleman Don Gurr, one of the best shots in the Army, who fought until his leg was

shattered (it was later amputated). Rifleman Murphy, also taken prisoner beside Brush, discovered an ancient Lewis gun which he got in working order and kept firing to the last round. These few held the enemy at arm's length for half an hour. Jerry Duncanson who had enjoyed every moment of it, stood up to kill the last German in the Rifle Brigade area, and himself died fighting. (25 May – British). (Group morale with desire for approval, increasing aggressiveness with suicidal traits).

25. Many wounded remained at their posts throughout the night and refused to go to hospital even after they were captured. So strong were regimental feelings that some had to be taken out of the prisoner-of-war column by the Germans for treatment, even when they had been on the march for days. (May – British). (Group cohesion and fear of the unknown).

Stamina and Exhaustion (Quotations)

26. The 24th [of May] had been a day of great tension. Not a great deal of fighting had been done by the Rifle Brigade nor were many casualties incurred, but the noise of the bombs, artillery, automatic weapons and sniping: the fantastic stories put about by enemy agents: the abandoning by the French of the forts and above all the fact that no commander ever had a moment to look around him and think and plan for more than the immediate future, all tended to intense fatigue. (British). (Noise, rumours, mistrust of foreigners).

27. Fatigue, thirst and the need to do the right thing, made it difficult to think clearly as I reached the railway embankment. (24 May – British). (The difficulty of decision-making under stress).

28. For many of the garrison the constant noise and heat and the need to hold vital positions, at whatever cost, became the first consideration. By the morning of the 25th [of May], lack of sleep had dulled their senses to everything except fighting the Germans. As the struggle raged at the canal front and in the harbour, the men led by their officers became more aggressive and daring. They thought only of killing Germans and by the end of the battle took suicidal risks in the hand-to-hand fighting. (British). (Increasing aggressiveness).

29. The exhausted Territorials fell asleep where they halted. They had had no rest since their departure from Kent on the night of the 21st [of May]. They had to be roused one by one when new orders arrived

during the night. (24/25 May – British). (Exhaustion after 4 days without rest).

30. They ['B' Company of the Q.V.R.] had already been without sleep for nearly four days, and yet they were fighting hard. (25 May – British). (4 days without sleep).

31. By nightfall, the defenders were very weary. Colonel Miller said that the 60th were 'cheerful but very done'. Allan described the position of the Rifle Brigade as 'far from happy'. Both regiments had made a remarkable stand and every clerk and cook was now in the line. (25 May – British). (4 days without sleep).

Firepower (Quotations)

32. A reason for the relatively low casualties for such a fierce battle was that many bombs and shells buried themselves in the sand dunes without causing injury. (May 1940 – British). (Experience of enemy fire).

33. A steady hail of tracer bullets and some tank shells came flying over the hump of the Pont Jourdan railway bridge. They bounced off the paving stones in all directions as I clung for life to the walls of houses on the side of the boulevard and crept towards the bridge. This was my first experience of street fighting and I was acutely frightened. It was difficult to understand how others could remain so collected under fire. Throughout the battle, the noise was so great that if you were more than ten yards away it was impossible to understand what was said to you. (24 May – British). (Fear during 'baptism of fire' and noise).

34. As it grew dark, with two patrols missing, the tank crews crawled into shell holes near the Gare Maritime. The noise of bombs, artillery, automatic weapons and sniping had all made for intense weariness. (24 May – British). (Noise and exhaustion).

35. As others have experienced, the sound of a single rifle shot, close at hand, was far more frightening than the stream of heavy machine-gun bullets in the boulevard. (24 May – British). (Experience and lack of concern over distant firing).

36. The 60th, lying without cover in the streets, had little protection from the Stukas. No one who experienced the attack on the morning of the 26th [of May] is ever likely to forget it. A hundred aircraft

attacked the Citadel and the old town in waves. They dived in threes, with a prolonged scream, dropping one high explosive and three or four incendiary bombs. They machine-gunned the streets and dropped a few heavy bombs between the 60th headquarters in the Rue des Maréchaux and the docks. Each of this series of attacks lasted twenty-five minutes. The first effects on the defence were paralysing but, as others had experienced with Stukas, the damage was moral rather than physical. Within a few minutes the riflemen eagerly fired Bren guns and engaged the Stukas, one of which was brought down on the seashore.

But the air attack hit the 60th in Bastion II and round the Citadel especially hard. The French, under de la Blanchardière at Bastion II, lost three officers and many men killed in a single raid. (25 May — British). (Fear, and its paralysing effects, increasing aggressiveness, experience).

37. The ship's departure had nothing sinister about it. Ironside himself confirmed ... that 'non-fighting' personnel and the wounded should be sent back as soon as possible ... But the return to England of half the Rifle Brigade transport was a blunder understandable only in the conditions of heavy shell fire. (24 May — British). (Fear and confusion under fire).

38. At 9 p.m. German aircraft made a dive-bombing attack on this bastion (Bastion 2), and machine-gunned it. They caused no casualties among the Q.V.R., but shot up their own troops in the wood on the side of the canal. But the attack led to confusion among the Q.V.R. as they withdrew and in the dark they lost their way. (25 May — British). (Fear and confusion under fire).

39. The Q.V.R. platoon at Bastion 7 ... had a particularly unpleasant time and were pinned down for several hours by machine-gun fire ... It was at this time that Corporal Burlton was killed in a gallant attempt to recover a Bren gun. For the moment the platoon were unable to move. (24 May — British). (Increasing aggression with suicidal traits).

Units (Quotations)

40. The two regular infantry battalions fought brilliantly ... The Tanks and the Territorials [battalions with a large proportion of reservists] bravely supported them to the end. (May — British). (Value of training and experience).

41. The regular infantry battalions, the 60th Rifles and the Rifle Brigade suffered the worst. Their casualties in killed and wounded were at least sixty per cent of their strength. (May 40 − British). (Casualties).

42. The division which Schaal commanded [10th Panzer] had already suffered losses and breakdowns on its long journey from Sedan. When it reached Calais it was at a little over half its strength. (23 May − German). (Casualties).

43. In his last message ... Allan reported ... 'Rifle Brigade casualties may be 60 per cent stop Being heavily shelled and flanked but attempting counterattack ...' (25 May − British). (Casualties and stamina).

44. Eden [Secretary of State for War] knew that, when he appealed, as he did in the later stages of the battle, to their past [the 60th Rifles and the Rifle Brigade], they would not fail to respond. And even if many ordinary riflemen never read his messages, they knew instinctively what to do. It may be fashionable today to sneer at regimental loyalty. Calais could not have been held for so long without it. (British). (Group cohesion).

45. Small detachments continued to defend houses in this area after being surrounded, and Platoon Sergeant-Major Stevens (16th Platoon), with some sixteen men of 'I' and 'C' Companies, having fought until all their ammunition was exhausted, hid in the houses round their positions for fourteen days before starvation forced them to surrender. (May/June − British). (Group cohesion with fear of the unknown and hope).

Leadership (Quotations)

46. On the platform of the Gare Maritime Keller [Commander of the Third Royal Tank Regiment] encountered a Full Colonel to whom he reported the arrival of his battalion. The Full Colonel replied that it was nothing to do with him as he was getting out with his kit as soon as the ship sailed. Like many others the Colonel had proper authority to leave for England as part of the evacuation of the noncombatants ordered by the War Office. Nonetheless this was a shock for Keller. (22 May − British). (Need for leadership).

47. He [Keller] had no transport and, finding the Full Colonel's staff car, he dumped the luggage from it on the quay, and, with his

adjutant, drove into Calais. (22 May — British). (Increasing aggress-iveness leads to ruthlessness).

48. I [Lt Neave] was ordered to join the Rifle Brigade and, with a party of gunners, set off ... I thought of others who had moved up into the line. This was it. Everything before was of no consequence. But would I pass the test? Such was my chief anxiety as I plodded down the Rue Mollien. (24 May — British). (Fear of failure with desire for approval).

49. I [Lt Neave] was conscious that, standing where I was, I could be of little use except to encourage the Searchlight men as they fired bravely, but inexpertly, towards Boulogne. (24 May — British). (Desire for approval, trust and subtle coercion).

50. On this day [25th May], Nicholson [C.O. Calais] twice refused demands to surrender. He was confident that his own brigade and their anti-aircraft supporters would fight whether or not evacuation took place at a later stage. He travelled long distances encouraging the men in the front line. (25 May — British). (Group and subtle coercion).

51. Nicholson believed that his presence at the Citadel with the two most senior British and French officers in Calais, would stiffen the resistance. He therefore, endured the most appalling bombardment which shook the old battlements of Richelieu and Vauban for hours on end. He was in constant danger of capture ... (25 May — British). (Group morale and group cohesion).

52. All my researches show that, in the disappointment and frus-tration of the hopeless battle, he [Nicholson] remained splendidly calm. He inspired confidence in those nearest to him, especially the French. (British). (Group morale and leadership).

53. They [the refugees] seemed about to rush the road-block, guarded only by the sergeant and a dim militia man. I drew my .38 Webley revolver ... and asked for silence ...
    I explained the situation in Calais and at length they agreed to stay in the fields. (23 May — British). (Coercion).

54. 'I [Keller] was very concerned how I was to get there. It appeared from Major Bailey's report that the Germans were already enveloping Calais from the south-east. A column ... must be coming up rapidly

and my only chance was to try and pass ahead of it – trusting that the column already south-east of Calais were only advanced guards.' (23 May – British). (Hope).

55. At 10 p.m., I [Lt Neave] arrived at the Porte de Marck, shaken by the bombing of Boulogne and my narrow escape. After the long journey on foot up the Route de St. Omer, I had been able to find some of my own troop. I was nervous and footsore but I tried to appear unbowed. (23 May – British). (Fear and group morale and the desire for approval).

56. 'I am afraid they may break through,' he said. ['B' Company Commander Major Poole with several First War decorations for gallantry] I was very surprised at the anxiety in his voice. 'Get your people in the houses on either side of the bridge and fire from the windows. You must fight like bloody hell.' (24 May – British). (Fear and experience).

57. Carlos de Lambertye was a French naval officer of the old school who believed in duty and discipline. It was clear to him that if Fort Lapin and the other bastions on the seafront were simultaneously abandoned, the Germans could surround and capture the Citadel before the end of the day. He knew of General Fagalde's orders that there was to be no evacuation. He determined to ignore the naval tugs with their orders to go to Cherbourg and keep back as many French sailors as possible to defend the bastions ...

Many of the men were already aboard the tugs at 3 p.m. ... de Lambertye addressed the men: 'Many of my sailors have already been killed or wounded. I need men to defend the forts. Who will volunteer?' ...

At first, only one man stepped forward at de Lambertye's question – this was Capitaine Michel de la Blanchardière, a staff officer of the 21st French Infantry Division. He was badly wounded ... Other French soldiers and sailors who had not embarked, now followed de la Blanchardière's example and remained on shore. De Lambertye told them bluntly: 'We must be ready, gentlemen, unless something quite unexpected happens, to fight to the death'. (24 May – French). (Group morale, subtle coercion and desire for approval).

58. It was about 3 p.m. that I [Lt Neave] arrived in the Boulevard Léon Gambetta. When the *Kohistan* [the last ship from Calais to England] had vanished, Green Jacket officers asked for reinforcements

from the crowd of soldiers and their officers sitting unhappily on the banks of the Bassin des Chasses de l'Est. It was now time to forget evacuation and show what 'non-fighting' soldiers could do. Fifty volunteered to go with me to the west of the town. They formed up behind the Gare Maritime and marched along the dock road as far as the Hôtel de Ville. Once under the determined glance of Green Jackets, not a man faltered. It would never have done to be seen to be afraid even though the shells were now coming in fast over the harbour. (24 May – British). (Group morale, hopelessness and leadership, subtle coercion and desire for approval).

59. At the Place Richelieu, Lord Cromwell, firing a Bren gun, was three times wounded that morning. He had already shown all those qualities that add up to real leadership in war. He was hit by bullets in both arms and in the head, the sight of one eye being badly affected. And yet he remained in command when all men at his barricade, save himself and two riflemen were dead. At 11.30 a.m. he was compelled to fall back to the line of the Rue des Maréchaux. (25 May – British). (Group morale, desire for approval, self discipline).

The Battle for Stalingrad

BACKGROUND

On 22 June 1941 Operation 'Barbarossa' commenced, and the German Wehrmacht attacked the Soviet Union. The end of the first year of the war was promising for the Germans. Four million Russian soldiers had been captured, Moscow and Leningrad were under siege, Kharkov was in the hands of the attackers, and Russia appeared to be about to collapse.

Early in 1942 the harsh Russian winter and a counter-offensive prevented any further advance, and later the over-committed and over-stretched German army no longer had the strength and resources for a renewed offensive on the previous year's scale. Therefore, Hitler concentrated on the southern part of the front with the aim of capturing the Caucasus oil. Initially, the German 'Blitzkrieg' technique was successful again, but then the German Army divided their effort between the Caucasus and Stalingrad, an important industrial town on the Volga and a vital transport centre. This resulted in a splitting up of the forces and afforded the enemy the opportunity to attack the weakly held left flank.

THE BATTLE

At the end of August 1942 the German forces reached the outskirts of Stalingrad, an industrial giant with a population of 600,000 stretching for 25 miles along the west bank of the Volga. The Germans, as if hypnotised, tried desperately hard to occupy the city using all their resources. The Russians on the other hand decided to defend it stubbornly and to the last man, because for them it had become the critical point of a bigger operation. This situation led to a battle which lasted in total for over 5 months, and for 70 days the German 6th Army fought inside the Russian encirclement.

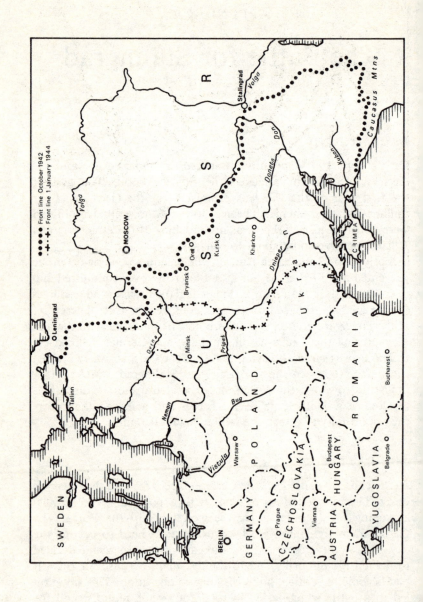

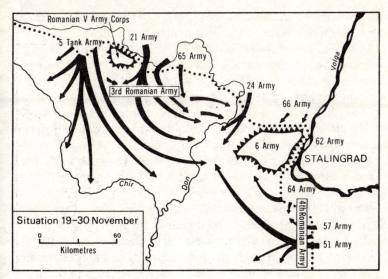

In mid-November the Russians held only three small pockets on the west bank of the Volga. The largest was about six miles long, but all of them were only a few hundred metres deep. On 20 November they started a wide encirclement operation from the north and south and on 23 November were able to close the trap on the German 6th Army with 22 Divisions comprising 364,000 all ranks. Hitler, against the advice of his staff, strictly forbade the breakout of the 6th Army. In December a major relief operation was launched from the south, but it failed. The 6th Army faced annihilation by enemy fire and from illness, starvation and the cold. On 2 February 1943 the battle was over. Out of 364,000 originally in the Stalingrad 'pocket' about one third were captured. Most of the others were dead.

PRESSURES

General Pressures (Author's summary)

For the German, Italian, Hungarian and Romanian troops the battle took place many thousands of kilometres from home. For the Soviet forces it was a matter of defending their homeland.

The core of almost all of the German units was made up of

experienced soldiers, while all the other nations had to make extensive use of men with little or no battle experience.

In spite of some reverses at the end of the first and the beginning of the second year of the campaign against Russia, the Germans had so far been very successful. The Soviets had had to put up with one reverse after another and could list as successes only a few defensive operations such as their determined retention of Leningrad and Moscow.

The attacking army was an allied one, while the defending army received only material support from its allies.

Extensive fighting at close range and house-to-house was a novel experience for both sides and placed a heavy burden on the fighting men.

The hitherto unknown massive deployment of artillery by the Soviets was also new (6000–7000 guns in the Stalingrad area).

Both sides, but the Germans especially towards the end of the battle, were hampered by hunger and cold owing to supply difficulties. In January German soldiers actually starved or froze to death.

Both sides had difficulty in looking after their wounded and recovering their dead.

In sum, the pressures at Stalingrad can be realized by studying the almost inconceivable number of dead. At least one million, but very probably more than two million people of many nations died at Stalingrad. This is more than at any other known battle.

Pressures on the Individual (Quotations)

60. When ordered into Stalingrad, Petrov went to the dock and saw that the other shore of the Volga was a solid wall of flames. Though scared to death, he knew he would go across. But other Russians would not, and Petrov watched as NKVD guards [People's Committee of Internal Affairs] fired in the air over the deserters, and then killed them when they ran from the landing. After Alexei climbed on board the barge, the NKVD took no further chances. Guards lined the rails to prevent anyone from jumping overboard.

Bombers came over, seeking out the steamers and tugs. German mortars behind Mamaev reached out for them, and Petrov cursed the slowness of the voyage ... Feeling trapped and vulnerable, he crouched down to hide from shrapnel singing by his ears ...

His boat took nearly two hours to reach a landing site under the cliff. While the dead covered the deck, the living scrambled off. Nearly half of Petrov's regiment had died crossing the river.

Because most of his unit was already dead, he now had to fight as an infantryman. His baptism to war was brutal. Three scouts went ahead to gauge German strength. Two came back. Petrov picked up his field glasses and scanned no-man's-land for the missing man.

He was out there, spread-eagled on the ground. The Germans had thrust a bayonetted rifle into his stomach and left him face up in the open. Petrov and his squad went berserk. Screaming hoarsely, they jumped from their holes and ran forward. Bursting into a line of houses, they killed anyone who rose before them. When several Germans raised their hands in surrender, Petrov squeezed the trigger of his Tommy gun and killed them all. (22 September – Russian). (Fear, cohesion, increasing tension, hate and revenge).

61. The thirty three were the last remaining wounded at an assembly point south of Gumrak. It made one sick to see the people who had come in just the way that they had been released from the battle. And here stood the last aircraft. This was the chance for survival. Is it not understandable that men crowded round the door, trying to get in, pushing and shoving? The body of the aircraft could accommodate sixteen men. When they had got in, eight more pushed in after them, and still there were nine left in the freezing solitude. They arranged themselves in the aircraft, lay on the floor, crouched, held on to struts and bars, literally lay on top of one another, and still there were six outside. And these six had to get in, so they threw out the stretchers, containers and the emergency lighting and took coats from wounds large enough to take a man's fist. They crept into the cockpit, sat in the tail turret, and still three men were not inside. Then they threw the ammunition out of the door, and the surgical dressings, and yet another man joined the living cargo that filled the metal walls right up to the roof ... The last man but one now stood on top of three of his comrades at the door, which would not close ... Now no one could have got in, even if they had scraped the paint off the walls. Outside, in the snow ... lay the thirty-third man with his knees shattered ... Do you know what it means to get a last chance of survival, when you are only twenty-two, when you have not washed for six weeks and have not had anything to eat except a piece of dry bread, raw turnips and boiled snow ...? No, you do not know and therefore you cannot judge the merit of the decision of the lance corporal from Iserlohn who was standing at the door above the three. He jumped out and went over to the last man and said: 'Both my arms

are broken, but you can't walk'. And so a few others clambered out, lifted him up and laid him right across the heads and shoulders of the others ... There is no other known case of an aircraft doing a lap of honour for an individual soldier. (January – German). (Group cohesion and group morale).

62. The moment that the post arrived is indescribable. This hotch potch of letters and cards shrank the miles from home ... For the soldiers, the war had stopped in an inconceivable, non-violent manner. (German). (Cohesion with relatives and escape from reality).

63. From the beginning of the encirclement, German military censors outside the *Kessel* had kept careful watch on the mail flown from Pitomnik to Germany. At first, the monitors estimated that more than 90 per cent of the letter writers exuded both complete confidence in their leaders and in their own ability to endure hardships caused by temporary reliance on the airlift. Also, because they had been involved in other temporary 'cauldrons' in the lightning-fast panzer actions of past years, German troops had had little difficulty relating those 'defeats turned to victory' to the predicament they faced at Stalingrad ...

That conviction had held until Christmas. Between that day and the end of the year, however, censors noted a sharp decline in morale ...

Still, the majority of the Germans in the *Kessel* seemed to retain a spirit of defiance and hope, or so they told their loved ones. One man wrote: 'Our weapons and our command are the best in the world.' Another boasted: '... we gladly make every sacrifice for our country in hopes that our people will see better times than we do.' A third said: 'Of course we will always be the stronger ones, there can be no doubt about that ...' In their mail analysis, censors flashed a warning signal to higher authorities about what to expect when January came: 'it must be expected that there will be a decline in morale as hope for relief ... wanes ...' 'The censors' prediction proved alarmingly accurate. An abrupt, fatal change in mood occurred, and the number of farewell letters increased dramatically ...

At Taganrog, German military censors analyzed the letters, sorted them into appropriate categories and forwarded a report on to Berlin and the Propaganda Ministry, where Dr. Joseph Goebbels read the findings.

1. In favour of the way the war was being conducted	2.1 percent
2. Dubious	4.4 percent
3. Skeptical, deprecatory	57.1 percent

| 4. Actively against | 3.4 percent |
| 5. No opinion, indifferent | 33.0 percent |

(December and January – German). (Change of motivation as hope dwindles).

64. There were also soldiers at Stalingrad, who behaved strangely ... Corporal Fehrmann had come from Brazil on 25 August 1939 at the last minute. He had an odd lot of luggage, a rucksack full of time-tables, maps, air tickets, shipping tables, travel brochures and a pocket globe. He was only marginally interested in the war. In the training battalion it had been noticed that he filled every spare hour preparing long journeys in great detail ... He had forty-nine complete travel plans in a folder ... He was just about to plan a journey through Vladivostok to Japan and the Philippines. At that very moment Ivan, or Konstantin, or someone with a similar name, three hundred metres above, pressed the bomb release ... Corporal Michel constructed clocks. Others ate, went shooting, wrote letters, collected money ... Corporal Michel constructed clocks. They were his passion ... His dugout looked like a museum. (German). (Escape from reality).

Injury and Death (Quotations)

65. In central Stalingrad, Sgt. Albert Pflüger, despite his broken arm, set up a machine gun to interdict some side streets, then sat back to think about the future. Fully aware that the Russians had already won the battle, he conjured up the possibility that Hitler and Stalin had reached an agreement on the humane treatment of prisoners of war. Pflüger also 'dreamed' that the Americans were going to intervene with Stalin to prevent the mass killings of captives.

These delusions helped immensely as he prepared himself for the ordeal he knew was coming. (January – German). (Continuation of the fight in spite of wounds, hope, flight from reality).

66. Corporal M. and his section lay in the snow in the front line. For days the Russians had been attacking with only tanks. They appeared in packs of five to eight tanks and drove straight into the deep echelons of the main defensive system. There had been no anti-tank activity for weeks. Then they sought out individual sections and with their tracks they crushed the men as they lay in the snow. The Corporal of 5th Company had watched this happening for four days, and in those four days he had seen nine of the groups in the vicinity wiped out. One day, when the attack was directed against his own men, he

gave in, left his own men in the lurch and disappeared. When the tanks had left, the battalion commander discovered the section of dead men … Next morning the Corporal lay in the snow next to the commander of the II Battalion. 'Good God, where have you come from, I thought you were dead'. Frightened eyes looked at the Major out of a haggard face. 'I simply could not stand the sight of men being brutally crushed to death. I know I have been a coward. I have just been to see my men. They were all dead'. The Major knew what it meant to be lying in the snow and seeing tanks coming towards you. 'All right. I shall not punish you and not court martial you … When it is dusk, go forward and take over Corporal Ziehrer's section. The company will not hear of this incident'. The following night the same terrible fate also befell Corporal Matthies and his group. (January − German). (Fear of being wounded and of death and overcoming it).

67. There were one hundred and forty wounded men at the post, all of them so seriously wounded that they could no longer fight. A hundred metres behind the fox-holes there was a dugout in a 'Balka' with eight wounded men. Each one had several stomach or head wounds. Although they were still alive their situation was hopeless. And then came the order to abandon the position. The Lieutenant passed on the order and added that all the wounded should 'withdraw' to the battle vehicles. This all went off well. Only the eight hopeless cases were still in the dugout, and there was no way to get them back. The company no longer had any stretcher bearers. There were only seven men in the foxholes, firing away and they had better things to do than drag away the wounded, because guns were aimed at them … But there was a doctor present, and the Lieutenant in charge of the company went to him: 'What are we going to do, doctor? I am not leaving any of those men in the dugout for the Russians'. And the doctor, who had a country practice in Lower Saxony, looked at the Lieutenant. 'In that case I shall stay here and hand them over to the Soviets'. The Lieutenant had a plan: 'You must be mad, because in that case we would not have a doctor any more. Give the men morphia, doctor, it would be merciful'. The country doctor looked horror-stricken into the company commander's blackened face. 'I must not. It's impossible'. The Lieutenant tried again to persuade the doctor. 'They are going to die in any case, all we can do is ease their death. The rules are simply different here'. The doctor looked down at the snow and shook his head. Time was getting short. There were

thirty minutes left to the time for withdrawal and firing was slowly dying down. It was hoped that the Russians would not notice and attack at once. The Lieutenant stood, battling with his conscience, but when there were only twenty minutes left he became calm. 'Doctor, I order you to give the men morphia and put them out of their misery.' Tears came to the doctor's eyes, then he turned and went back to them. Meanwhile the first of the neighbouring groups withdrew. The seven men in the foxholes came crawling back and when the last man had left the position the Lieutenant ran to the dressing station. The doctor was sitting there on a stretcher and in front of him lay eight dead German soldiers. (January – German). (Group morale).

68. While Münch [battalion commander in the 71st Division] clambered into the plane, Russian shrapnel sprayed the crowd. The pilot quickly gunned the motors and tried to lift off. He could not. Looking out of the window Münch saw nearly fifty men lying on the wings, holding on to anything they could ... as the Ju-52 picked up speed and raced down the strip. One by one, the riders fell off ... Shorn of its added burden, the plane rose swiftly into the bright sky and turned away from the Volga. Münch tried hard to calm himself. For the first time in more than two months, he could not hear the sound of guns. (January – German). (Fear of the unknown).

69. With the last hours at hand, wounded German soldiers in countless cellars asked for pistols, placed them to their temples and fired. (February – German). (Death wish and fear of the unknown).

70. In the early morning of January 24, General von Hartmann, commander of the 71st Division, ... led a small band of men out to a railway embankment. Standing upright in full view of the Russians across the snowfields, he shouted: 'Commence firing!' and shot a clip of bullets from his carbine.

Col. Günter von Below hurried from Paulus's cellar with the order to 'stop this nonsense.' But Hartmann ignored him and continued to fire at the enemy. Within moments, a Russian bullet tore into his brain.

A short time later, another German general settled his own affairs. Hearing that his son, a lieutenant, had been killed while trying to lead some men out of the city toward far-off German lines, General Stempel took out a pistol and shot himself in the head. (German). (Death wish).

Stamina and exhaustion (Quotations)

71. Hitler was besotted by the idea that any retreat must destroy fighting morale. He was unable to grasp the fact that a retreat enforced by the enemy must have a much more damaging effect than a regroupment based on one's own initiative, and this resulted in the sacrifice of entire divisions and corps in the last years of the war. (German). (Fear of failure).

72. North of the Don, the Russian forces continued their buildup. They moved at night, in long trains which came from the Moscow area and the Urals, carrying more than two hundred thousand troops ... Russian political officers worked tirelessly to infuse the troops with fanaticism. Each new soldier stood before the banners of his regiment and received his weapon in a formal ceremony. Martial songs were sung, and party officials read speeches on the need for devotion to the Motherland ... (Russian). (Motivation, group morale).

73. During Christmas Eve, the Stalingrad front remained alarmingly quiet. Little was heard from the Russians, except the squawking of loudspeakers urging the Germans to lay down their arms and come over to good food, shelter, and friendly Tartar girls. Crouched in their snowholes, German soldiers still listened with detached amusement to the propaganda. Most of them feared the Russians too much to trust such alluring proposals. (German). (Propaganda, fear of the unknown).

74. On December 31, ... a private first class, APO No. 24 836 B wrote: 'The Russians are flooding us with leaflets. When I come home I shall show you some of the nonsense that they are writing. They want us to surrender. Do they really believe we are puppets for them? We will fight to the last man and the last bullet. We will never capitulate. We are in a difficult position in Stalingrad, but we are not forsaken. Our Führer will not leave us in the lurch ...' (German). (Propaganda and hope).

75. Hour by hour, the *politrook* bombarded the Germans with announcements, threats, inducements, and prophecies. In some sectors, Russian speakers even called out the names of company and battalion commanders.

Capt. Gerhard Münch learned this when a commissar engaged him in a personal war. Near the Red October Plant, the loudspeakers blared over and over: 'German soldiers, drop your weapons. It makes no sense to continue. Your Captain Münch will also realize one day what is going on. What this "super-fascist" tells you isn't right anyway. He will recognize it. One day we'll seize him.'

Every time the enemy mentioned his name, Münch immediately went out and spent time with his troops. Joking about the personal comments, he watched closely for any adverse reactions from the men. But though the tactic was meant to be unnerving, they never seemed intimidated by the Russian ploy. (December, January − German). (Propaganda and group morale).

76. When a sergeant stumbled back to Rettenmaier's command post and demanded more grenades, a doctor looked at his bloodshot eyes and told him: 'You must stay here. You may go blind.' The sergeant refused to listen. 'The others back there can hardly see a thing, but we must have grenades.' Only when another soldier volunteered to take them did he slump into a chair and pass out from exhaustion. (Mid-November − German). (Group morale, stamina and exhaustion).

77. Rettenmaier also was facing an acute decline in morale. The half-rations his men ate did not alleviate their melancholy, and they missed their homeland most of all. Deprived of regular mail, they fell victim to forebodings of an inconceivable fate. Conversations dwindled to whispers in the shelters. Men sat on their bunks for hours, seeking solitude with their thoughts. They wrote letters at a feverish pace, hoping that airlift planes might carry their innermost sentiments to relatives waiting at home. (End November − German). (Fighting spirit, lack of food and news from home).

78. Thousands of men staggered from one defensive line to another. Sometimes these lines were many kilometres apart. Sometimes they existed only in the imagination of the general staff officers. But the men attacked tanks, took up position behind anti-tank and anti-aircraft guns, and fired as long as they had anything to fire with. There were others who hid in the ground, in the vehicle parks or in cellars. They only emerged when they heard German aircraft engines or when the rations were dropped. Then they stole whatever they could find and filled their bellies with sausages and bread. According to army orders, looters were to be shot in sight. In the area of the four divisions west and south of Stalingrad three hundred and sixty-four executions were carried out in eight days. The sentences were given for cowardice,

absence without leave, desertion, and theft of stores. Yes, theft as well. (January — German). (Fighters, 'passengers' and coercion).

79. Dr. Cristoforo Capone had been running for several days. When he came to the valley, he saw mobs of Italians rushing back and forth at the bottom of the deep gorge. Behind Capone, a Russian tank fired into the crowd, and an officer beside him suddenly gurgled as a rifle bullet went through his neck.

Capone broke away but had no place to hide as machine guns and artillery raked the valley floor. Soldiers toppled, blew into fragments, or stood resignedly, awaiting the impact of a bullet. Some officers and men raised their hands in surrender. Others refused. A surgeon Capone recognized, screamed: 'They're going to kill all of us!' and ran at a Russian machine gun that cut him to pieces. For a fleeting moment, Capone thought of doing the same thing, but to his right, another group of Italians suddenly put up their hands. He joined them, and while he watched the enemy approach, several officers in the line changed their minds, pulled out pistols and shot themselves. (23 December — Italian). (Stamina and death wish).

Fire-power (Quotations)

80. On that day ... a heavy barrage descended on a battery where 55 men had already been killed. It could no longer have any effect on the dead battery. When the tanks arrived, there was nothing left for them to do. The last two survivors were crouched on the edge of a crater ... (5 January — German). (Effect of fire against troops with inadequate cover).

81. On one occasion the main fighting line was withdrawn another 400 metres, but by 5 a.m. the front of the 60th Motorised Division had been broken and half an hour later the Russian tanks were in the rear of the 79th Armoured Infantry Battalion. Of the 16th Artillery Regiment one howitzer was still firing and the 16th Motorcycle Battalion was firing with infantry weapons until they had nothing left to fire. To the right of the breakthrough a barrage of fire passed over seventy men of the Motorised Division from Danzig and returned a second and a third time. Sixty-three men were killed. The seven survivors were caught by the fourth wall of fire half an hour later. (31 January — German). (Fire effect against troops with inadequate cover).

82. There were two other men who must be mentioned. It was in the northern blocking position near the Konoja railway station. They had fitted out their dugout well, as high as a man. It even had an adjoining sleeping quarter ... The front was quiet and the Russian positions were one hundred and fifty metres away. Now and again a shot was fired, otherwise nothing happened. It was about 1400 hrs. Suddenly there were a dozen explosions. The privates in the company and in the regiment were dozing or writing letters. Now they rushed out of their dugouts to peep over the top, but there was nothing in sight. Twenty minutes later there were more explosions, but again nothing could be seen ... That went on for three days. From 12 noon to about 1400 hrs., every twenty or thirty minutes. The reports said: 'Attack by rifle fire'. The company located the probable target and the battalion passed the report to the regiment. There was no doubt that the fire was directed against Post 135. On Saturday it happened again. Eight times for two minutes. Including the intervals this lasted for three hours. Then peace. The regimental commander crawled through the connecting trench and lay down near No. 135 for 15 minutes ... The battalion and company commanders followed at intervals. The R.S.M. did as well. A minute's silence and then the commander blew his top. He seemed about to have a stroke ... He yelled for three minutes ... Then he crept back. The battalion commander remained much quieter ... The company commander stood there, red-faced. The two lance corporals from 135 thought he was going to explode. When the battalion commander was fifty metres away he actually did explode – with laughter ... The two men of 2nd Company had thought up an amusing game out of sheer boredom. With clay they painted six circles on a steel helmet ... Then they bet on hit or miss, a Reichsmark a time, then they raised the helmet on a pole, 10 centimetres above the parapet ... Down with the helmet, check, pay out the winnings, fill in the hole, bet, out with the thing again. In Post 135 there were seven steel helmets completely shot to pieces. Lance Corporal Grube had won one hundred and sixty-four Reichmark. (German). (High spirits, humour).

Units (Quotations).

83. The tank no longer had any tracks, but it was possible to close the hatch, and the gun and machine guns were working. There were five men in the tank and they had made themselves as comfortable as possible. The tank had got stuck in the front line, and earlier, a

regimental commander had set up his command post in it. For this
reason there was also a telephone line to division. The regimental
commander had gone, so had his unit, but the five men who belonged
to a nearby regiment had settled in: 'To the end of the world'. They
tried out the machine gun, it worked. They swivelled the gun and
pushed a shell up the barrel, it made a bang. They found the telephone
and turned the handle, division answered. They hung up the receiver
and remained undetected by the enemy for a whole week. Until the
Russians attacked. The five let them come up to within fifty metres
and then held them up. That gave them 24 hours' peace. Next day
tanks appeared and things got stickier. They fired hopefully and
destroyed three T 34s. In the evening they passed a 'battle report' to
division. There was a distance of two kilometres between them and
the German front, and the Russians tried with mortars, then with
artillery and finally once more with tanks ... First, the five ran out
of machine gun ammunition, then they fetched the last crumbs of
bread from their greatcoat pockets and then they turned the handle
of the telephone and asked what they should do. Division could give
them no assistance but they did get a reply:
'Think of the Russians in the silo'.
The story of the 'Russians in the silo' is as follows:

> The 71st Infantry Division was attacking on all sides the grain
> stores which were being defended by Russian soldiers. After
> three days the defenders sent a radio message to their com-
> manders ...
> 'We have no more food'.
> The answer was 'Fight, then you will forget your hunger'.
> Three days later they transmitted again: 'We no longer have
> anything to drink, what are we to do?' and back came the reply:
> 'Now is the time comrades, to live on your wits and your
> ammunition'.
> The defenders waited for two days and then came the last
> message.
> 'We no longer have any ammunition'.
> Hardly five minutes passed and they had their reply:
> 'The Soviet Union thanks you, you have served your purpose'.

And that was what the five men in the tank were thinking of when
the last round had tossed an anti-tank gun four hundred metres away
into the air. They were powerless against flamethrowers. When the

sun rose, there was no one left to answer from Command Post 506 ... (January – German/Russian). (Group morale).

84. The wind blew from the north-east and the thermometer registered thirty-five degrees below zero. The men lying outside Stalingrad to the south and the west knew little or nothing about the situation. They were fighting for their lives. The II Battalion of the Grenadier Regiment 523, with 100 men was stationed towards the south. Food had failed to materialise for the fourth time. They dug a hole and covered over the dead with snow. The living were also rigid from head to foot. They crouched in the holes, the tent strips wound round their heads, their knees drawn up to their chins. They waited for the fire and the attack. The firing lasted two hours and buried the hundred men. There was no chance of defending themselves. 400 metres to the west the last of the men of Regiment 195 were no better off. Of the eighty men, fifty fell, the rest were dispersed or taken prisoner. The propaganda machine from the other side dropped leaflets. The message was: 'Come to us, comrades, stop this senseless carnage, you will be well looked after' ... however unlikely it seems, very few deserted to the other side. But they all kept their leaflets just in case! That is only one side of the story. Partial surrenders occurred everywhere. The units acted in accordance with the situation, but the men put up their hands only when they no longer had any ammunition in their pockets, or if they were standing in front of a T 34 and had the choice of either surrendering or letting themselves be crushed in the snow. (January – German). (Group morale, hope, fatalism, fear of the unknown).

85. Only a few days earlier, Wenck had received urgent orders to leave his post in the Caucasus and assume command of the 'screening' line in front of the Russians pushing southward toward Rostov from Serafimovich and Kletskaya.

Needing troops and equipment, the colonel instituted his own set of rules. He rode the highways and dragooned stragglers into ad hoc units. He played movies at intersections and when exhausted soldiers stopped to watch, Wenck brusquely marched them back to war. One of his noncommissioned officers found an abandoned fuel dump and put up signs reading: 'To the Fuel-Issuing Point'. Hundreds of cars, trucks, and tanks drove into this oasis only to become part of Wenck's new army. (November – German). (New units).

86. On 12 January there had already been a panic in Pitomnik. The supply units had fled simply because a single tank had broken through and was driving about the area. The Chief of the General Staff had fumed, put through a dozen long distance calls and by next morning the place had been retaken. (German). (Fighting spirit of the supply units).

87. In the early hours of 26 January, the GS02 of the 44th Infantry Division woke the C of S of the Corps: 'Colonel, the Romanians have deserted during the night. Disaster for the 44th'. Sad though it seemed, it was a fact. The regiment of one thousand and one hundred men, which had been entrusted with the defence of the area between the 44th Infantry Division and the 29th Motorised Division had surreptitiously disengaged itself from the front line. They had crossed over to the Russians during the night, taking all their arms and their equipment with them. It was discovered that this regiment had a telephone line to the Russians and was informed of all the attacks. (German/ Romanian). (Allies).

88. Other remnants of the Italian Army were trying to escape through a valley near the town of Abrusovka thirty miles to the west. But on the surrounding slopes, Russian gunners had installed the awesome *Katusha* rockets, which whooshed thousands of rounds of high explosives into the writhing gray masses on the valley floor.

A small German detachment trapped at one end of the cul-de-sac managed somehow to commandeer several trucks and enough fuel to make a run through the gauntlet. A few Italian soldiers attempted to jump on the running boards, but the Germans shot them. Other Italians who clung desperately to door handles had their fingers smashed by rifle butts. Having driven their allies back, the frantic Germans pulled away and disappeared in a southerly direction. (23 December – German/Italian). (Allies).

89. The Luftwaffe [German Air Force] has left us in the lurch, they have not kept their word. (18 January – German, General Schmidt, Chief of Staff of the 6th Army). (Arms of the services).

90. On the night of 2 February the remaining officers of the 16th Panzer Division met in the command post ... Twenty men stood there, unshaven and filthy with long beards and dirty bandages, with camouflage tunics, driving coats or anoraks. When the general arrived they saluted. 'Gentlemen, the battle is over. The 6th Army has ceased

to exist. We have done our duty to the last. Thank you. I release you from your responsibilities. At this moment you must all know what you have to do. Should any of you succeed in getting back to our own lines, give my love to the Fatherland'. The general shook hands with everyone and thanked each of them personally. Then, in his camouflage uniform he walked to the tractor factory. Lt. Brendgen went with him. 'Stay where you are, Brendgen. You must obey my order, even though it is my last'. And Brendgen saluted and saw the general disappear into the ruins. You cannot recognise a general among thousands of dead men wearing camouflage dress. (German). (Release from group cohesion and suicide).

91. On the evening of 25 February the staff of the Artillery Regiment of the 71st Infantry Division met in the regimental dugout. Each man drank a bottle of 'Schnapps', gave a cheer for Germany and shot himself on command. (German). (Alcohol and suicide).

Leadership (Quotations)

92. On this day ... hundreds of officers cursed the futility of the orders given, and yet they obeyed them ... the Chief of Staff of the LIst Army Corps stated: 'The situation is hopeless. Everyone may do whatever he wishes' ... General Stempel said to his son: 'Conduct yourself to the very end like an officer and a gentleman'. (5 January – German). (Group morale and fatalism, refusal to accept responsibility and self-discipline).

93. Just a few hundred yards west of Chuikov's ... headquarters, Capt. Gerhard Münch was faced with his first case of insubordination. It had been triggered by the Führer's 'Christmas Drive', the annual fund-raising campaign for the Nazi party that reached even into the *Kessel*.

One platoon from Münch's companies refused to make any donations. When he asked the reason, an officer said: 'Captain, you will have to see for yourself what is wrong.'

Münch went to visit the platoon, reduced to six men, and inquired about the trouble. The men told him they were no longer prepared to fight. One trooper added: 'Captain, I will no longer play the game. We are fed up!'

Stunned by their attitude, Münch wisely decided to say nothing. He sent the men to the rear and waited beside their machine gun until replacements came to fill the gap. Then he went to his command post, called for the rebels and told them they could sleep at his quarters that night.

In the morning, he shared breakfast with them, and as the group sat on the floor sipping hot coffee, Münch watched them carefully and noticed they seemed a bit more relaxed. Gingerly he brought up the previous night's difficulty. The rebels answered without hesitation.

The underlying cause of their mutiny was a letter from one of the soldier's wives, who had asked why he was at the front while several of his friends stayed at home. The soldier had been so upset that he had read the letter to his friends. It had driven them into a state of rebellion as they, too, began to wonder why they had to fight the war for malingerers in Germany.

Münch let them talk out their bitterness, then brought them back to reality. 'According to martial law, you are liable to punishment,' he told them. 'You know how refusal to obey an order will be punished. Are you prepared to return to your positions, and not desert or do foolish things? Can you promise that?'

They answered with a spontaneous chorus of yesses. One soldier went further, 'We will fight for you as long as you command the battalion. But if you are wounded or killed, we wish to be free to make our decisions'.

Münch considered the offer briefly, then chose to compromise. 'All right, confirm it by handshake,' he replied. 'As long as I command the battalion you will have to fight. Thereafter you may do what you want.'

The men shook hands with him on the bargain. (16/17 December – German). (Importance of the people back home, of sleep and food and of trust).

94. The brilliant fireworks display lasted for several minutes ...

It was their salute to the Holy Season, a joyous time to every German, and for several days, German officers and men alike had prepared feverishly for the celebration. Capt. Gerhard Münch even drafted a speech. At his command post in a cellar of the Red October Plant, he labored for hours to hone his message, then, in the early evening, he went to a nearby garage where a Christmas tree, carved from wood, adorned one corner of the cavernous room. In groups of thirty, his infantrymen appeared to sit around him as he welcomed them and distributed cigarettes, wine, or tea with rum, a piece of bread, and a slice of horse meat.

Relaxed by the liquor, the men listened attentively while Münch spoke quietly of the need for keeping up the fight against the Russians. Still slightly unnerved by his recent brush with the mutineers in the ranks, he took pains to underline a soldier's duty to orders, especially in such a dreadful situation as at Stalingrad. The pep talk seemed to appeal to the troops, who all joined in singing *'Stille Nacht'* ('Silent Night') with him. Münch noticed that in midchorus, a number of men were so choked with emotion they had to stop singing and wipe tears from their eyes.

After talking personally with every enlisted man, Münch went back to the Red October Plant to drink with fellow officers. (24 December – German). (Motivation by pep talks and group cohesion as a result of celebrating together).

95. As Kästle issued final instructions before sending them off to battle, one soldier broke down completely. Sobbing hysterically, he clutched at the lieutenant and begged to be spared. Kästle talked urgently to him, trying to quiet his fears. The man listened and then, while the column started to march off, he wiped his tears away and ran to take his place in formation. (January – German). (Fear and motivation by pep talks).

96. A battalion led by Captain Mues ..., reached the Volga, and turned north ... Fog and a light snow began to obscure vision but the aggressive Mues pushed on. Fearless, revered by his men as 'immortal', he was tracked by a Soviet sniper, who put a bullet in his brain. The attack stopped abruptly as Mues's troops gathered around the stricken officer, now unconscious and near death. They ignored the bullets and cried over the man they loved.

An officer from another regiment finally came, lifted Mues in his arms and staggered away with the heavy burden. Soldiers who had fought with the captain through Russia broke down and collapsed. Others became fearful and timid as news of his death spread like a bushfire. (16 November – German). (Desire for leadership).

97. Inside the perimeter of the newly arrived Soviet 64th Division, stationed twenty-five miles due north of Stalingrad, morale was particularly bad. A German air raid had levelled the field hospital, killing many of its nurses and doctors. Wounded men back from the battlefield told horrifying stories of enemy superiority, and

these tales spread fear among the inexperienced troops. They started to slip away singly, in pairs, and finally, in large groups.

With the division on the verge of dissolution before ever seeing combat, its commanding officer acted decisively to curb the epidemic. Calling a general assembly of regiments, he stood before them and berated them for shirking their duties to the Motherland. The colonel charged his men with the same guilt as those who had already run off and told them he intended to punish them for cowardice.

His harangue ended, the colonel moved purposefully to the long lines of massed soldiers. A pistol in his right hand, he turned at the end of the first row and began counting in a loud voice: 'one, two, three, four.' As he reached the tenth man, he wheeled and shot him in the head. As the victim crumpled to the ground, the colonel picked up the count again: 'One, two, three ...' At ten, he shot another man dead and continued his dreadful monologue: 'One, two ...'.

No one bolted. Nurses standing beside the formation sucked in their breath at the macabre scene. The colonel's mournful voice stabbed at the troops, '... six, seven ...' Men mentally guessed their place in line and prayed the colonel would finish before he got to them. When the last bullet in the revolver thudded into a man's brain, the commander shoved the pistol back in his holster and walked away.

An officer bellowed, 'Dismiss!'

The order ricocheted across the parade field, and soldiers broke from formation and scattered in all directions. Behind them six of their comrades lay in a neat pattern on the grass. (27 August – Russian). (Coercion).

The Battle for Monte Cassino

BACKGROUND

In the first three years of World War II, the Axis Powers achieved a number of resounding victories in Poland, France, Norway, Denmark, Russia, Greece, Yugoslavia, the Mediterranean and North Africa. But in the second half of 1942 they suffered their first serious setbacks. These were highlighted by their defeat in El Alamein/Alam Halfa in September 1942, which finally led to their retreat from Northern Africa in May 1943 and the defeat and loss of the German 6th Army in Stalingrad in February of the same year.

The tide had changed in favour of the Allies, which in the Mediterranean theatre of war led step by step to:

9 July 1943	–	Allied landing in Sicily.
3 September 1943	–	Clandestine armistice between Italy and the Allies.
	–	Allied landing on the Italian mainland (Reggio).
9 September 1943	–	Allied landing in Salerno.
29 September 1943	–	Unconditional surrender of the Italian Armed Forces.
13 October 1943	–	Declaration of war by Italy on Germany.

After the landing of the Allies in Reggio and the defection of the Italians, the Germans decided to delay the Allied advance and to take up a strong defensive position south of the Apennines. By this they hoped to gain the time needed to repulse attacks expected from the Italian Forces and to reorganize their own forces in order to take over the areas given up by their former ally. However, the situation for the Germans developed rather better than they expected. The Italian Forces posed no major problem. The advance of the invaders was rather cautious and it was hampered by bad weather and supply

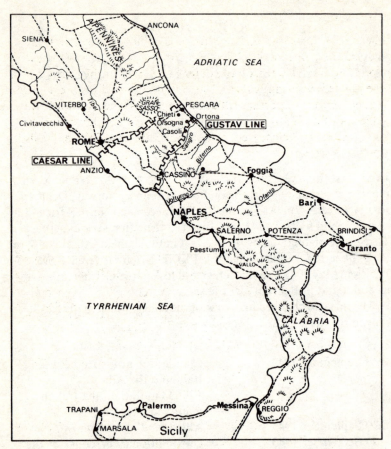

difficulties especially for the British divisions. Therefore, the Germans
decided to take advantage of this and Field Marshal Kesselring, the
German commander, ordered in the last days of September the
construction of an additional defensive system in the extremely
suitable area on the general line of the Garigliano–Mignane rivers,
the Volturno–Majella mountains, and the river Sangro. One of the
pivots of the system was the old and famous monastery of Monte
Cassino, which overlooked and commanded Route 6, the Via
Casilina, the 'Gateway to Rome'.

THE BATTLE

For the Germans this was the fifth year of the war. The fighting in Italy had already lasted for more than four months. The failures were mounting. For this reason the defences on this freshly constructed line gained in significance. The intention was to prevent the psychologically important Allied advance on Rome. In addition, the Allied Air Forces, which were already putting considerable pressure on the German Reich, were to be denied the use of the airfields in northern Italy.

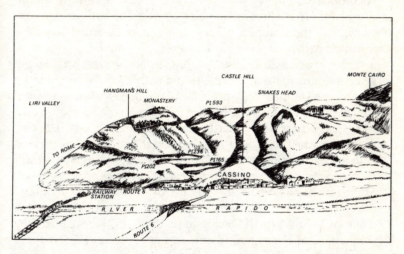

It took the soldiers of the United States of America, Canada, Great Britain (New Zealand, India, Cyprus, Nepal), France (Algeria, Morocco) and Poland six months to break through these defences. Historians tend to differentiate between the following battles:

17 January–12 February 1944	First battle for Cassino.
(22 January–	Allied landings at Anzio and Nettuno)
15 February–17 February 1944	Second battle for Cassino.
15 March–23 March 1944	Third battle for Cassino.
11 May–20 May 1944	Fourth battle for Cassino.

On 9 June 1944, three days after their landing in Normandy, the Allies at last reached Rome. The German forces continued their fight in Italy right up to the end of the war in May 1945.

PRESSURES

General Pressures (Author's summary)

At the outset, the majority of the formations deployed could rely on soldiers with battle experience, but owing to the heavy losses many had to be replaced during the battle by inexperienced men.

The Allies had almost unlimited superiority in the air and at sea.

The German troops were able to fight from well-prepared positions, making use of high ground dominating the surrounding terrain.

Artillery and bombers were used to an extent not known before in World War II. In Stalingrad there were greater artillery concentrations, but the bomber attacks in Cassino exceeded anything experienced earlier.

The lack of adequate reserves on the German side resulted in some large formations fighting for months on end. Thus for instance the 1st Parachute Division fought for 220 days almost without respite.

The battles all took place in snowy and wet conditions.

The greater part of the battle area was mountainous. Lack of vegetation made it difficult to find cover, the hard rock prevented the quick construction of proper positions and the rugged terrain made observation easy and permitted enfilade fire almost everywhere.

Some results could be achieved only by hand-to-hand fighting.

Several historians have called the battle for Monte Cassino the 'Verdun of World War II' owing to its duration, the weather, the determination of the opposing armies, the firepower involved, the system of defences and the number of casualties.

Pressures on the Individual (Quotations)

98. The order to move arrived at noon ... it gave us an hour to be ready ...

We knew the message well. It had happened so often. It was routine. In this case we had been expecting it for three days. Nevertheless one always experienced a feeling of slight sickness when it did arrive. It had the finality of the starter's 'get ready' in a race. It was the footstep of the warder to the man in the condemned cell ...

You made the usual wan little jokes. The others did the same. And no one was deceived ... You knew they were all thinking: 'Oh Christ!' (April – British). (Fear before the attack).

99. The new men who would be going into action for the first time wondered how they would stand it and tried not to show that this was what they were wondering. The ones who had survived many actions wondered how long their luck could hold, and these concealed their feelings behind a jocularity that was often forced. The best unit commanders went out of their way to wander informally among their men that day, and to talk with most of them. The more anxious ones took refuge in aloofness ... Most of them wrote a letter. The one which begins 'Don't worry if you do not hear from me for a while ...'. All day long they busied themselves ... But by the afternoon everything had been done ... There was nothing left now but to wait for it to begin. That was when the tension began to be felt ... (May – British). (Fear before battle and fear of failure).

100. It would be foolish to imagine that the average British or American soldier went into battle thinking he was helping to save democracy. It is safe to say that he never gave democracy a thought. He went into battle because battle had become the whole of his life, his job. (May – British). (Motivation).

101. We all knew what the *Gestapo* had done in Poland ... It is not surprising that we welcomed the opportunity to be revenged on the Germans. (Polish). (Hatred and revenge).

102. ... one was conscious of the feeling of high comradeship which binds a man with fierce intensity to those with whom a profound and fearful mission has been shared ... It is the fighting man's reward. (British). (Group cohesion through common experience).

103. The light was good because it meant comparative safety and rest. The dark was bad because it meant no safety, no rest, and it hid the danger. The dark always brought with it the fear of counter-attack. (British). (Fear of the unknown and the unexpected).

104. Being attacked by night is particularly unnerving because you cannot tell if there are twenty of the enemy or a whole battalion. (British). (Fear of the unknown and the unexpected, in this case fear of the dark).

105. You can never have an easy night when there is nothing between you and the enemy. And the more tired you are the greater is your fear of counter-attack. (British). (Fear of the unknown, in this case of the dark and increasing with growing exhaustion).

106. If two machine-guns can infiltrate through your positions and open fire from behind, the most dogged temperament finds it hard to resist the impression that it is surrounded. We had ourselves on several occasions successfully employed this technique and taken a large number of prisoners ... (British). (Fear of the unknown and the unexpected).

108. The soldier becomes less conscious that he is living in an insect-ridden cave by filling it with photographs and pin-up girls and labelling it 'the Ritz'. (British). (Self-discipline and humour).

107. You must never acknowledge that abnormality exists. Once you do the whole structure of morale is bound to collapse. (British). (Self-discipline).

109. One is forced, in such places, to squeeze laughter out of the simplest matters. Normal standards of humour, like normal standards of everything else, cease to apply. (British). (Self-discipline and humour).

110. I have found that when civilized living has to be temporarily suspended, there are three hygienic essentials to one's well-being: teeth, shaving, and nails − in that order ... A shave, as the Army has always known, works wonders with one's morale ... Filing the nails − apart from considerations of cleanliness − I have always found to be an admirable occupational therapy when I was very frightened. (British). (Self-discipline and cleanliness).

111. Then the conversation would broaden. From 'I wish I had a base job in Naples' to 'I wish I had a base job'. It is the infantryman's safety-valve ...
   Not that the casual visitor from the other world would notice it. It is put away, when visitors come, because it is something personal and intimate within a unit ... (British). (Fear and hope in conflict with group morale).

112. Operational existence is much easier to tolerate when you have a definite clear-cut objective. (British). (Fear of the unknown).

113. There's nothing like a good breakfast before you fight. (British). (Food).

114. Then there was a clatter of machine-gun fire from the direction of the right-hand company ...

There was nothing for it but to 'Stand to' and await developments ... It might be the start of an offensive − or it might be a fighting patrol ... The tension of total alertness temporarily eclipsed one's tiredness. Nobody spoke, ...

... then the firing ... was definitely easing off ... everyone simultaneously sensed the easing of the tension. People began to talk again. They made the rather forced little jokes which follow a period of fear ... One suddenly felt very, very tired. (British). (Fear, increasing and decreasing tension as tiredness comes and goes).

115. There was nothing we could do but wait and hope that the situation outside would improve ... 'We were dying to know exactly what was happening up on Hill 593, but we could not send out scouts to what would have been certain death. We dragged the wounded to the back of the cave, flung ourselves flat as far as possible from the opening and prayed for reinforcements to arrive.' (11 May − Polish). (Fear, inactivity and hope).

116. We had lost all sense of time. (11 May − Polish). (Sense of time).

117. You lose even the vaguest sense of time. You take your objectives and dig in, and then you go on again ... (British). (Sense of time).

118. If only we could have seen clearly what was happening, we should have felt better, but we were largely dependent on information reaching us by word of mouth. (11 May − Polish). (Information).

119. Our companies were now inextricably mixed and many of us were losing heart, but we clung together in small groups and continued to harass the enemy. (11 May − Polish). (Group cohesion and fear of being isolated).

120. In the first light of dawn I spotted a low wall ahead of us. At the same moment there was increased sniping activity and we lost a number of men because they started taking unnecessary risks. For instance, one of them ran across to the wall and calmly perched himself astride it, although a German machine-gun was blazing away at us. He received a direct hit that ripped out his insides ...

Most of us were content to huddle ourselves in the holes and hollows we had found ... (11 May − Polish). (Passivity and increasing aggressiveness with suicidal tendencies).

121. The psychological value of hitting back is enormous in defence. (British).

122. Some commanders prefer to sit back in their defences and avoid stirring up trouble ...

John was allergic to quiet sectors ... he'd suddenly jump up and say, 'Couldn't we let the mortars have a go at something ...?' (April – British). (Activity).

123. I turned to the other lieutenant, who was crouching down on the far side of the cave, and remarked resignedly, Well, that's that! The company up there has pulled out. He eyed me desperately, peered outside and then, without warning, he charged out of the cave and rushed for cover behind the nearby rocks. Dozens of machine-guns stuttered briefly. He rolled over and lay still. Another man, who ran out almost on the heels of the lieutenant, was also hit and badly wounded.

For a while nobody moved. We were listening tensely to the rattle of the machine-guns and the exploding of grenades. It was as though we had been frozen into immobility. The spell was broken by one of our heavy machine-gunners. He had one hand-grenade left. Abruptly he stood up, pulled out the pin, leaped out of the cave and let fly. The explosion followed almost immediately. Hit in the chest, the machine-gunner staggered back and collapsed only a few yards from me. Water! he gasped hoarsely. Water, please! Then, with a convulsive jerk, he died. (11 May – Polish). (Resignation, then increasing aggressiveness with suicidal tendencies).

124. Soldiers, even when wounded, are reluctant to retreat. We stayed where we were and sought the best cover we could find ... (11 May – Polish). (Exhaustion and passivity).

125. Today we were relieved quite unexpectedly. It does not appear to be a good thing, for it comes too suddenly, but the main thing is that we get out of these hills. (17 March – German). (Fear and relief).

126. The first reaction, when you know you are to be relieved, is simple, straightforward joy. You feel an overwhelming affection for the people who are going to relieve you. (April – British). (Fear and effects of being relieved).

127. So we passed into the third phase of reaction that precedes relief. You suddenly felt very impatient. You wanted to get away quickly. Fear long suppressed, came to the surface. (British). (Fear and effects of being relieved).

128. It is not until the ordeal is over and someone says: 'Well done. You've nearly finished now'. It is not until then that your mind relaxes, and for the first time you are really conscious of how intolerable your lot has been. (British). (Relaxation of tension with exhaustion).

129. Where was it the officer had said they were going? ... Half of them didn't remember, nor did they care. All they knew was that they were on their way 'out of it' ... And after they had slept they'd ... get into a town. It didn't matter which town. Any town would do. Where there were streets to walk in and shops and cafés and women. Above all they wanted women. They didn't necessarily want to sleep with women. They just wanted ... To hear women's voices, and hear them laugh, and talk to them and tease them. (British). (Relief from fear).

Injury and Death (Quotations).

130. Most of the killing you do in modern war is impersonal. A thing few people realize is that you hardly ever see a German. Very few men — even in the Infantry — actually have the experience of aiming a weapon at a German and seeing the man fall. There is a lot of loose talk about the use of the bayonet. But relatively few soldiers could truthfully say that they had stuck a bayonet into a German. It is the threat of the bayonet and the sight of the point that usually does the work. The man almost invariably surrenders before the point is stuck into him.

 With modern weapons ... this impersonal killing has become quite scientific business. (British). (Fear of death and mutilation).

131. The death of Jenkins upset everyone for quite a while ... It is always like that with a solitary death. The death of one always affects you more strongly than the death of many. (April — British). (Fear of death and a feeling of guilt).

132. They buried Jenkins the same evening, and the padre read the burial service. The Pioneers made a fine cross ... They spent a long time working on Jenkins' grave, ... (April — British). (Fear of death and a feeling of guilt).

133. We drove on past the wayside graves, past the red cross vehicles bringing the wounded back from the place where we were going. And deep in our hearts we envied the wounded. Lucky wounded. You

thought of the peace and quiet to which those wounded were going. You thought of a clean hospital bed. And it seemed the most wonderful and desirable thing in the world to be wounded. (April – British). (Fear of death and group morale).

134. The *Goumiers* are hawk-faced Moroccan troops whose speciality is mountain fighting ... though they will consent to carry rifles, they prefer their knives ... They had a habit of bringing back evidence of the number of victims they had killed, which made them an unpleasant enemy to face. (May – French). (Fear of mutilation).

135. Listening to their technical chatter, it was amusing to compare their respective Artillery slang ... American gunners, too, have their picturesque way of paraphrasing their lethal intentions. (British). (Attitude to killing).

136. In the meantime Baade [who had assumed command of the 90 Armoured Infantry Division on 14 December 1943] had also established a small rest centre for members of his division. At the discretion of the commanders ... a few soldiers could be sent there for short rest periods. If necessary and in case of an alert, a speedy return to their unit was assured. In addition, Baade had also made arrangements for lightly wounded soldiers to receive medical attention in this rest centre. In that case, unlike being sent to hospital in Germany, they were sure of being able to return to their unit ... (German). (Group cohesion of wounded men).

Stamina and Exhaustion (Quotations)

137. You can endure anything if you know when it is going to end. (British). (Hope of relief from fear).

138. When men are undergoing a great strain, and it begins to wear them down, they must have a moon to reach for. This need was fulfilled by the city of Naples. Naples was the nearest embodiment of the Other World. It became the symbol of every man's immediate aspirations. It became a fixation. (British). (Hope of relief from fear).

139. The performance of the 34th Division at Cassino must rank with the finest feats of arms carried out by soldiers during the war. When at last they were relieved by the 4th Indian Division fifty of those few who had held on to the last were too numbed with cold and exhaustion to move. They could still man their positions but they could not

move out of them unaided. They were carried out on stretchers ... (11 February – American). (Endurance).

140. Some of our troops were still attempting to scale Hill 569, only a mere eighty yards or so distant. We should have already gained control of that feature, but unfortunately we were too far below strength to launch a successful attack. All I recollect is that the dead were fixing us with unseeing eyes, no matter in which direction we looked. We were fast approaching the end of our tether. We no longer knew where to shoot or whom to aim at. We were mentally blank, stupefied, exhausted. Thoroughly disorganized as we were, with scores of officers and men dead or dying, we badly needed reinforcements. (11 May – Polish). (Utter exhaustion on the first day of attack).

141. Shortly before dusk a young staff officer of the brigade we were to relieve arrived to take us forward. He spoke in the strained, jerky, trying-not-to-show-it way of men exhausted by prolonged operations. He seemed so worn out it made one feel guiltily fresh. (April – British). (Effects of exhaustion on behaviour).

142. The other lieutenant, who was trembling with shock, implored me to withdraw, but I insisted that we were all right. In spite of contradictory evidence, I still clung to the belief that we had control of the hill-top. (11 May – Polish). (Effect of exhaustion and hope on the leader's decision).

143. By night they manned their positions fully. By day, while concealed sentries kept watch, the others rested in neolithic dwellings, ... (April – British). (Rest).

144. Every forty-eight hours one of the forward companies was relieved by the reserve company. During its period in reserve, a company made up for the limited battle menu with a succession of enormous hot meals in the gully. (April – British). (Food and rest).

145. At the same time he [Major-General Baade] demanded above all that good food should be provided. He checked the field kitchens himself and demanded that every private should have at least one good meal a day. 'Eating just soup makes one cowardly' he said ... (German). (Food).

146. The word 'leave cancelled' is itself damaging ... And even if only three men in a company are on leave, those three are happy and three others are happy at the prospect of going on leave soon ... (December – German). (Fear and relief from fear, hope and recovery).

Firepower (Quotations)

147. The remarkable thing about modern shelling is not how many it kills, but how few. These constant exchanges of fire, however, were far from being a sedative to the nerves of men who were more often than not wet and cold, getting no proper rest ... (British). (Effect of firing on soldiers).

148. Tensely we waited in our holes for the bombs to drop. Then they came. The whining scream of their approach, the roar of their explosions and the noise of the aircraft themselves mingled with echoes flung back from the hills to produce an indescribable and infernal bedlam of noise. The whole earth quaked and shuddered under the impact. Then – a sudden silence. Hardly had the dust settled a little than I dashed out to visit the other two strongpoints ... From somewhere a voice shouted: 'All's well!' and then the next great wave of air hulks loomed into view above me.

I could not go back. I remained where I was, and the flood-gates of hell opened once again. We could no longer see each other; all we could do was to touch and feel the next man. The blackness of night enveloped us, and on our tongues was the taste of burnt earth. 'I'll come again', I said, felt my way towards the exit and rolled out into a crater. I had to grope my way forward as though in a dense fog, crawling, falling, leaping; as I reached my post, another wave was on the way in. The men pulled me head over heels into our hole. Then down came the bombs again. A pause, and once more I groped my way across the tortured earth. Direct hits – here, here and here; a hand sticking out of the débris told me what had happened. When I got back, the men read in my eyes what I had seen. The same, unspoken thought was in all our minds – when would it be our turn? The crash of bursting bombs increased in intensity. We clung to each other, instinctively keeping our mouths open. It went on and on. Time no longer existed, everything was unreal. We shifted our positions and, well, we thought, if we can still move, we're still alive – sixteen of us.

Rubble and dust came pouring down into our hole. Breathing

became a desperate and urgent business. At all costs we had to avoid being suffocated, buried alive. Crouching in silence, we waited for the pitiless hail to end. (15 March − German). (Fear, noise, paralysis).

149. Thunderous explosions brought me leaping from my bed. At the dugout entrance stood a runner, who shouted that fifty or sixty Lightnings had dropped bombs. The thought flashed through my mind: 'This is it!' As I was about to jump out of our cellar, the runner yelled: 'Look out! More of them!' and as he yelled the first bombs began to fall. Outside it must have been absolute hell. The bombing went on and on. There was nothing we could do but crouch tense and expectant, where we were. Then came a brief pause ... or could it, we wondered, be the end of this inferno? Corporal Kübrich, commanding a mortar section, jumped down into my cellar. He had streaked here like a hare − but he was only just in time. The whole town had been completely obliterated, he reported. Instead of having to make the usual detour, he had been able to make a bee-line for my battle headquarters. He was anxious to go on to his own section's position, but that, for the time being, was quite impossible. Bombs were now falling like rain, and in our underground shelter the thought struck me that we were just like a submarine crew whose U-boat was being pursued by depth-charges.

Then came a longer pause. 'Two volunteers to go to X and Y positions!' I shouted. At once my trusty lance-corporal, Jansen, and a runner from No. 8 Company sprang towards the exit. Jansen had just got clear away, when another explosion blew the other runner back into the cellar. In rapid succession a number of bombs fell very close, and one scored a direct hit on the forward exit of the cellar. Luckily the front of the building collapsed slowly, and we were able to escape into the rear part of the cellar; but a good number of our weapons and some of our ammunition were buried under the debris.

The entrance to the cellar was completely blocked, and we were cut off. By the light of a flickering candle we sat among the ruins and glumly took stock of the situation. After a while the explosions seemed to be a little more distant. 'Let's get cracking,' I shouted, 'and clear the entrance! We must get out of here!' We set to work, clawing at the mass of rubble and earth. We lost all sense of time, and how long we worked I don't know; but we seemed to be making no impression, and it looked as though we should never get out; some of the men began to lose heart, and I, too, was hard put to it to overcome an inner feeling of helplessness. At last we seemed to be making progress, and then the rubble and earth outside came sliding down and undid all that we had done. 'Never mind – stick it!' I shouted, 'We're not going to die here, like rats in a sewer!' Once again we started to claw away, and after hours of labour we cleared a small cleft. But here, solid masses of masonry, beyond our strength to shift, barred further progress. We shouted to attract attention, and our shouts were heard by two runners from Battalion Headquarters, who were out looking for us. With their help, we cleared the entrance, and after being buried alive for twelve hours, we squeezed our way out into the open. Darkness had now fallen. Cassino was unrecognizable in the tangled mass of ruins and rubble that confronted us ... (15 March – German). (Effects of firepower on soldiers).

150. The last bomb fell at twelve-thirty p.m. At that precise moment, the artillery opened fire. The curtain was rising on the second act. The artillery of three corps – the New Zealand, the U.S. II and the French – joined by Eighth Army artillery and the batteries of the British X Corps set about the task of crushing the last shreds of German resistance. By three-thirty, zero-hour for the combined infantry and armour attack, 746 guns had fired nearly 200,000 shells on the town and hill, a weight of metal corresponding roughly to 1,300 lorry-loads ... General Heidrich and Colonel Heilmann ... were convinced that nothing could survive.

The Allies were of the same opinion. Six senior generals, among them Alexander, Eaker and Clark, had watched the whole fearsome spectacle from Cervaro. To them it was obvious that the New Zealanders and Indians were bound to capture their objectives ...

And, indeed, no one could have believed that after such a tornado there would still remain one single German soldier capable of offering resistance. By all human standards, the fighting spirit of such para-troops as had not been buried beneath the ruins must surely have been shattered to a degree that would render them incapable of any further endeavour ...

Men had died everywhere, and the attack had wrought terrible havoc in the ranks of the 2nd Battalion, 3 Parachute Regiment. The day before the attack it had mustered about 300 men and five guns; now at least 160 men and four assault guns lay buried beneath the ruins. Worst hit of all had been No. 7 Company. Only a mere handful had survived the onslaught of guns and bombs, only then to find themselves cut off; and few indeed succeeded in fighting their way back to their own lines. The other companies had been reduced to fifteen or twenty men apiece, and only No. 6 Company had escaped without loss. At the beginning of the air attack it had been with the battle headquarters, in reserve in the cellars of a large business house. In the pause that had followed the first wave, Captain Foltin had transferred his staff and No. 6 Company to a rock cavern at the foot of the monastery hill – a move that spelled salvation for him and defeat for the New Zealanders!

The latter had advanced gaily and for the most part in close formation to the outskirts of the town; the tank commanders were standing upright in their turrets as though on a ceremonial parade. They were the first targets of the German snipers, and over many a tank commander his turret crashed closed for the last time in his life.

As the last shells burst and the barrage passed on to search the depth of the German positions, the paratroops, gaunt-looking, in tatters and covered with dust, crept out of their holes and took post behind the nearest remnant of wall they could find. Of their prepared positions no vestige remained. (15 March – German). (Effects of firepower on soldiers).

151. Shells from our own artillery were screaming over our heads in sporadic bursts. The Germans were blasting away, too. Tension, as might be supposed, was inexorably mounting. Zero hour was rapidly approaching, but my men, with one notable exception, were not afraid. The only man whose nerve broke was a young corporal who begged me leave him behind. I understood exactly how he was feeling, so I granted his request. He survived that action, but destiny had evidently marked him for her own, for he was killed later on in the battle.

At eleven that evening the desolate countryside was intermittently illuminated by a bewildering succession of bursting shells. The barrage was tremendous. Apart from eleven hundred pieces of artillery, there were the mortars and anti-tank guns blazing away. We could feel the ground trembling and were conscious of the quivering air. I personally was very much aware of the thumping of my heart.

Conversation amidst the thunderous rumbling was completely out of the question. The noise deafened us. We had no idea how long this artillery preparation would last, but I for one felt that if it went on for long I should go mad. In point of fact, we endured the threat to our eardrums for three-quarters of an hour. (11 May − Polish). (Noise and fear).

152. All we could do was lie down and pray. For forty-five minutes the barrage was concentrated on our positions. Men were wounded and killed, but there was nothing we could do about it and nobody could help us.

Then, just as we were thinking we could endure no more, the firing suddenly stopped. We decided to take a chance. (11 May − Polish). (Effect of firing on soldiers).

153. When the first attack started, the Germans replied with a tremendous barrage ...

I saw one cadet wounded in a manner that illustrates the state of mind most of us were in. A shell exploded right at his feet, and when I went to examine him I felt confident I should find a dead body. To my intense surprise, he had sustained only a few minor bruises. He was so dazed, however, that when he stood up he mechanically withdrew the pin from the hand-grenade attached to his belt. After the explosion he was so badly wounded that he had to be sent for prolonged treatment ... (11 May − Polish).

154. When my O.C. congratulated me and said I ought to go out again as observer for the Brigade, I am not ashamed to admit that I turned pale and wet my trousers. I think I was still suffering from the effects of that barrage from the hills. (13 May − Polish).

155. The Poles had certainly expected the artillery preparation to have yielded better dividends. The barrage had made little impression on the German infantry, especially on those dug in on the reverse slopes of hills where only direct hits would have been effective. The counter-battery bombardment had failed to silence the enemy's artillery and mortars and damaged communications had been rapidly repaired. On the other hand, the German shelling had almost immediately severed Polish communications, more particularly those of the 5th Wilno Brigade, and the consequent confusion had led to a complete lack of control in the assault. (May − Polish). (Effects of firing on soldiers, equipment and communications).

156. On March 15th the Allied Command had psychiatrists standing by to examine the first prisoners that came in to see what effect the bombing had had on them. It was assumed that there would be many

cases of nervous collapse. The paratroops, mostly boys in their teens or early twenties, seemed to know what was expected of them. When they were asked about the bombing they forced a smile, shrugged their shoulders and said that it was nothing. Their attitude was that of a schoolboy who, emerging from the Headmaster's study rubbing his behind, defiantly informs his friends: 'It didn't hurt'. Of the first three hundred prisoners to come in, only one was found in a nervous condition directly attributable to the bombing. (German). (Effects of bombing of soldiers).

157. One thing the New Zealanders quickly found out: The U.S. Air Force had presented the Germans with a first-class tank obstacle: The towering piles of rubble, the torn and debris-strewn streets, the innumerable deep bomb craters made it quite impossible for the New Zealand 4 Armoured Brigade to penetrate into the town and support the infantry ... It took the pioneers thirty-six hours to clear a narrow corridor to the centre of the town; and through a narrow gap of that nature it was quite impossible to launch a tank attack. (15 February – New Zealanders). (Effects of built up areas).

158. A shell bursting on ordinary ground partly buries itself (and some of its effect) and directs its blast and shrapnel forward. A shell or mortar bomb bursting on the flint-hard slope of a mountain had a much more damaging effect, and the fragments of metal flew farther and less predictably. In addition the troops were denied, as we have seen, the normal cover of trenches as these could not be dug into the rock. (British). (Effects of firing on rocks).

159. The hard digging earlier in the morning is paying a good dividend. The last three salvoes landed right on our mortars, but they are well dug in and they get away without a single casualty. (May – British). (Effect of fire on trench).

160. Among the measures taken by the Germans during the night to hamper the crossings was to blind the river banks with smoke on a very large and concentrated scale. This had the effect of nullifying the moonlight and adding considerably to the confusion and difficulty which in any case attends a river-crossing operation. (11/12 May – German). (Effect of smoke).

161. When you have been fighting for a long time you develop an instinct for enemy observation-posts. You spot quickly where they

must be, and you seem to know intuitively the exact moment you start being watched. And it is like suddenly being stripped of your clothes. (April − British). (Effect of being observed).

Units (Quotations)

162. There is no difference between the great offensive and the small battle except of degree. All battles are small groups of men fighting other small groups until one or the other can fight no more. (11 May − British). (Importance of the size of an operation).

163. The N.Z. Division was in the best sense a great amateur combination − a gifted civilian body that had learned the craft of war the hard way, and now excelled at it. (New Zealand). (Self confidence and self reliance).

164. They [the New Zealanders] had two other attributes invaluable to the infantryman. They were self-reliant and well able to act independently. Many of them were men who single-handed had run remote farms or sheep stations, a way of life that teaches a man to think and act for himself without relying on the facilities and assistance of others. They were for the same reasons natural improvisors ... (New Zealand). (Self confidence and self reliance).

165. Behind the superficial casualness the division [the New Zealanders] had a hard practical discipline conditioned partly by the constant scrutiny of their activities from 'back home' and partly by a ruthless system of removing any man who failed in his job. They set themselves high standards, and those who failed did not keep their jobs. (New Zealand). (Influence of relatives and of personnel selection).

166. If a New Zealand paper announced that the New Zealanders were fighting at Cassino, every second family in the country would directly or indirectly be concerned.

The effect of this, coupled with the confident character of the men themselves, was almost to compel the New Zealand Division to take itself for granted as a *corps d'élite*, forced always to excel. If a man did well it would for a certainty get back to his home town or village. If he did badly it would get back too. (New Zealand). (Influence of relatives).

167. The 78th were perhaps the most sophisticated division in the two armies. They had fought continuously through North Africa, Sicily,

and Italy. They had never known defeat. They had developed a tremendous *esprit de corps* ... (May – British). (Experience, success and *esprit de corps*).

168. We paired off with our opposite numbers in the Polish advance party and showed them around ... We got along very well together, though they could never wholly conceal their slight impatience with our attitudes. They hated the Germans, and their military outlook was dominated by their hate. Their one idea was to find out where the nearest Germans were and go after them. It was praiseworthy, but often unpractical. (April – Polish). (Influence of hatred on decision making).

169. They [the Poles] thought we [the British] were far too casual ... They didn't perceive ... that we were, in fact, as serious as they were. Nor did it occur to them that in a modern war, which depends so much on cool calculation and elaborate and careful planning, ours is the kind of temperament to have. This was clearly borne out by results. The Poles always had much heavier casualties than we did, largely because of their impetuous way of setting about a battle. (British/Polish). (Impetuosity and its effect on the conduct of operations).

170. The forward company [5th Kresowa Division] had run out of ammunition and the Germans were mounting a counter-attack, but even at this moment of crisis Polish morale remained as high as ever. The men actually began hurling stones at the enemy and kept up their spirits by singing the national hymn. (17 May – Polish). (Group morale and national fervour).

171. But to assert that the defenders of Cassino, these paratroops 'rotten with Nazi-ism', had performed this unique feat of arms simply and solely because of their ideological outlook, is nothing but ... an excuse with which to cover up a military blunder. It could with equal justice be asserted that the Allied Commandos owed their impressive feats to their fundamental outlook on life. Would anyone care to attribute the stubborn defence of Bastogne to the fact that the American paratroops must have been particularly fanatical democrats? The values which gave Heidrich's paratroops the strength and ability to stand up to the onslaughts of the Fifth Army were different. The secret of their success can be summed up in three qualities – comradeship, *esprit de corps*, efficiency. Those were the foundations

of every *corps d'élite*. The word comradeship looms large in the vocabulary of the German parachute arm.

Nor does it do so fortuitously. It was inevitably inherent in the character of this corps of specialists, composed, up to 1944, exclusively of volunteers. When paratroops go into action, officer and man sit side by side in the same aircraft, the officer is the first to jump — and lands as often as not in the midst of the enemy. He runs the same risks in jumping and is in the same danger of being shot while coming down as his men; he lands on the same hard ground and is just as likely to suffer broken bones as they are. His haversack contains the same modest rations, his water-bottle is filled with the same thin coffee as theirs ...

They knew that exceptional feats of arms were always expected of them, and they did their utmost to prove worthy of the confidence placed in them. And so it was at Cassino. To the men of the 1 Division to surrender town and hill to the enemy was unthinkable. The high repute of their division was at stake, and to preserve that no sacrifice was too great. They were determined to defend Cassino until they could fight no more.

Fighting spirit alone, however, cannot achieve everything. Behind it there must be sound military knowledge and training. (German). (Group cohesion, group morale, professionalism).

172. There was an indication of their mentality [the paratroops] during the German counter-attack on Castle Hill which turned the tide of the battle. After the first ferocious assault down the mountain-side had been held, a sergeant-major and half a dozen lightly wounded paratroopers surrendered to the Castle garrison. When the second German attack came in all except one, the sergeant-major, volunteered for duty as stretcher-bearers. They worked very hard and constantly exposed themselves to danger. One even saved the life of a British officer by jerking him out of the line of fire of a sniper. While the battle was raging — the attackers were getting right up to the walls of the besieged castle courtyard — the sergeant-major watched the proceedings with a dispassionate professional eye, almost as though he were an umpire. When it was all over (and it was a particularly unpleasant close-quarter fight) he approached the senior surviving British officer, congratulated him in formal terms on his handling of the situation, and asked him to accept his Paratrooper gauntlets as a token of his admiration. It is difficult to explain this attitude, except

as a product of an indoctrination and discipline so complete, that once capture is an accomplished fact — and, through injury, unavoidable and therefore honourable — a man instinctively welcomes the nearest available discipline because he cannot get along without it. (German). (Group morale, laws of the group and discipline).

173. But Captain Beyer [1 Parachute Division] could do no other than stay behind and await capture. He had lost a leg in the battle of Cassino.

General Rudnicki ... asked ... 'How was it possible for you to put up with these conditions for so long without surrendering?'

The German replied, 'We had our orders to fight as long as we considered it necessary. We were NOT commanded to fight to the death. We simply hung on till the last minute. We were also told that the Poles did not take prisoners'. (17 May — German/Polish). (Group morale and fear of the unknown).

174. We began to experience again that sense of being on top of the job which every seasoned fighting team knows. The feeling that this was one of the hardest nuts you ever had to crack, but the early, difficult stage has now been successfully overcome, and once again the old gang has come out on top ... It is this spontaneous consciousness of collective skill and devotion that causes one battalion to do better than another, though both are composed of equal numbers of more or less equivalent Englishmen, armed with identical tools of war. It is deep and satisfying and compensates you for the unpleasant things. (British). (Professionalism, success and pride).

175. There was, however, a more humane side to the picture. The exceptional closeness of the combatants, together with the restriction it imposed on daylight movement, led gradually and spontaneously to the practice of openly evacuating wounded men in daylight under the Red Cross flag. Nothing was arranged officially. It was done sparingly. But it was done, and both sides respected the Red Cross. It was one of those situations in which front-line soldiers, separated by a hundred yards or less, seem to develop a strange kinship in extremity. In the mountains the stretcher-bearers of both sides made these occasional daytime excursions into the boulders and thickets of no-man's-land, and sometimes they exchanged words with one another. (Codes of conduct).

176. The lines were always going ... somebody had to go out, find the break, and mend it. This duty was carried out by the regimental

signallers ... They were ordinary private soldiers ... Theirs was the dangerous task of maintaining the telephone lines in the very forward areas ...

They got no extra pay for it. But they wore on their sleeves two little crossed flags, the badge of the signaller, and they were rather proud of it. (British). (Group cohesion and pride in outstanding performance).

Leadership (Quotations)

177. At a time when operation orders were inclined to become great wordy dossiers of foolscap, packed with administrative detail, Montgomery preferred the direct briefing. He would personally brief as many officers as possible. He would summon a meeting of all concerned down to, and including, battalion commanders and say, in effect: 'All we have to do is this, that, and the other thing'. The battalion commanders would return to their units completely clear about what was to happen, and what they personally had to do. They would repeat what they had been told to their own officers – on many occasions commanders would assemble their entire battalions and brief the whole lot. The consequence of this was that a Montgomery operation always began with everyone knowing what was to happen, why it was to happen, how it was to happen, and what his own job would be ... (British). (Information and motivation).

178. There was one other unique feature of this division. This was what the New Zealanders themselves called their 'Cabinet'. The cabinet consisted of Freyberg [CO of Division] and the senior brigadiers, and when an operation was being prepared plans would be fully, and even outspokenly, debated. Freyberg would listen carefully to everyone in turn, then sum up and make the final decision. These cabinet meetings constantly mystified British and American generals ... (New Zealand). (Team work, information and motivation).

179. It was not only a hard battle for the ordinary soldier. It was also a testing time for Commanders ...

I must say that every Polish eye was fixed on our Corps Commander, General Anders. Always calm and confident of victory, he was a source of inspiration to all of us ... And this faith spread to the humblest private. (Polish). (Faith in the commander).

180. He thought it essential [Baade] to change several of the commanders. If he thought that he detected an inadequate ability and steadfastness in some senior officers during the battle for Ortona ... he saw to it ... that they were replaced. (December − German). (Personnel selection).

181. And knowing that he must be in full view of the O.P. that had directed that fire, Sergeant Mucky started to make his way down that precipitous boulder-strewn slope, carrying the one who was badly wounded over his back, and aiding as best he could the two that could walk. (British). (Group morale, leading by example, compassion).

NOTES

1. Neave, *The Flames of Calais*, p. 34.
2. Neave p. 37.
3. Neave p. 93.
4. Neave p. 34.
5. Neave p. 36.
6. Neave p. 99.
7. Neave p. 158.
8. Neave p. 159.
9. Neave p. 95.
10. Neave p. 103.
11. Neave p. 109.
12. Neave p. 124.
13. Neave pp. 126-7.
14. Neave p. 155.
15. Neave p. 16.
16. Neave p. 15.
17. Neave pp. 154-5.
18. Neave p. 167.
19. Neave p. 131.
20. Neave p. 131.
21. Neave p. 127.
22. Neave p. 128.
23. Hastings, *The Rifle Brigade*, p. 18.
24. Neave p. 201.
25. Neave p. 171.
26. Neave p. 131.
27. Neave p. 117.
28. Neave p. 139.
29. Neave p. 134.
30. Neave p. 151.
31. Neave p. 162.
32. Neave p. 20.
33. Neave p. 117.
34. Neave p. 123.
35. Neave p. 124.
36. Neave pp. 190-1.
37. Neave p. 94.
38. Neave p. 168.
39. Neave p. 97.
40. Neave p. 17.
41. Neave pp. 20-1.
42. Neave p. 69.
43. Neave p. 169.
44. Neave p. 77.
45. Hastings p. 20.
46. Neave p. 48.
47. Neave p. 48.
48. Neave p. 65.
49. Neave p. 126.
50. Neave p. 139.
51. Neave p. 140.
52. Neave p. 67.
53. Neave p. 67.
54. Neave p. 52.
55. Neave p. 84.
56. Neave p. 118.
57. Neave p. 110.
58. Neave p. 116.
59. Neave p. 191.
60. Craig, W., *Enemy at the Gates*, pp. 104-5.
61. Schröter, H., *Stalingrad*, pp. 214-5.
62. Schröter p. 228.
63. Craig pp. 311-13 and 361.
64. Schröter pp. 221-2.

65. Craig pp. 360-1.
66. Schröter pp. 212-13.
67. Schröter pp. 211-12.
68. Craig p. 55.
69. Craig p. 371.
70. Craig pp. 366-7.
71. Schröter pp. 102-3.
72. Craig p. 149.
73. Craig p. 291.
74. Craig p. 312.
75. Craig p. 324.
76. Craig p. 226.
77. Craig p. 226.
78. Schröter p. 210.
79. Craig pp. 276-7.
80. Schröter p. 247.
81. Schröter p. 281.
82. Schröter pp. 223-4.
83. Schröter pp. 227-8.
84. Schröter p. 257.
85. Craig p. 214.
86. Schröter pp. 200-1
87. Schröter p. 237.
88. Craig p. 276.
89. Schröter p. 202.
90. Schröter pp. 281-2.
91. Schröter p. 252.
92. Schröter p. 246.
93. Craig pp. 243-5.
94. Craig pp. 286-7.
95. Craig p. 322.
96. Craig pp. 172-3.
97. Craig pp. 71-2.
98. Majdalany, *The Monastery*, p. 9.
99. Majdalany, *Cassino: Portrait of a Battle*.
100. *Cassino*, p. 232.
101. Connell, *Monte Cassino*, p. 175.
102. Monastery p. 77.
103. Monastery p. 77.
104. The Monastery p. 64.
105. The Monastery p. 113.
106. The Monastery pp. 64-5.
107. The Monastery p. 67.
108. The Monastery p. 67.
109. The Monastery p. 67.
110. The Monastery p. 25.
111. The Monastery pp. 52 & 54.
112. The Monastery p. 96.
113. The Monastery p. 100.
114. Monastery pp. 64-5.
115. Connell p. 188.
116. Connell p. 182.
117. Monastery pp. 90-1.
118. Connell p. 182.
119. Connell p. 185.
120. Connell p. 185.
121. Monastery p. 44.
122. Monastery pp. 38-9.
123. Connell pp. 188-9.
124. Connell p. 161.
125. Cassino p. 210.
126. Monastery p. 67.
127. Monastery p. 70.
128. Monastery p. 68.
129. Monastery p. 76.
130. Monastery p. 57.
131. Monastery p. 63.
132. Monastery p. 64.
133. Monastery pp. 12-13.
134. Cassino p. 249.
135. Cassino p. 61.
136. Von Plehwe, F. K., *Reiter, Streiter und Rebell*, p. 258.
137. Monastery p. 47.
138. Monastery p. 52.
139. Cassino p. 87.
140. Connell p. 183.
141. Monastery p. 14.
142. Connell p. 187.
143. Monastery p. 22.
144. Monastery p. 23.
145. v Plehwe p. 248.
146. v Plehwe p. 229.
147. Monastery pp. 29-30.
148. Böhmler, *Monte Cassino*, pp. 210-11.
149. Böhmler pp. 211-12.
150. Böhmler pp. 212-14.
151. Connell p. 180.
152. Connell p. 161.
153. Connell p. 168.
154. Connell p. 160.
155. Connell p. 136.
156. Cassino p. 214.
157. Böhmler p. 136.
158. Cassino pp. 206-7.
159. Monastery p. 108.
160. Cassino p. 244.
161. Monastery p. 12.
162. Cassino pp. 241-2.
163. Cassino p. 102.
164. Cassino p. 97.
165. Cassino p. 101.
166. Cassino pp. 96-7.
167. Cassino pp. 247-50.

168. Cassino p. 168.
169. Monastery p. 68.
170. Connell p. 143.
171. Böhmler pp. 242-4.
172. v Plehwe pp. 214-15.
173. Connell p. 152.
174. Monastery pp. 36-7.
175. Cassino pp. 207-8.
176. Monastery p. 45.
177. Cassino pp. 41-2.
178. Cassino pp. 101-2.
179. Connell pp. 173-4.
180. v Plehwe pp. 227-8.
181. Monastery pp. 69-70.
182. Connell p. 158.